FARGO

FARGO

Behind the Glitz and Glamour

SCOTT NANKIVEL

iUniverse, Inc.
Bloomington

Fargo
Behind the Glitz and Glamour

iUniverse books may be ordered through booksellers or by contacting:

iUniverse
1663 Liberty Drive
Bloomington, IN 47403
www.iuniverse.com
1-800-Authors (1-800-288-4677)

*Because of the dynamic nature of the Internet, any web addresses or links
contained in this book may have changed since publication and may no longer be
valid. The views expressed in this work are solely those of the author and do not
necessarily reflect the views of the publisher, and the publisher hereby disclaims
any responsibility for them.*

*Any people depicted in stock imagery provided by Thinkstock are models,
and such images are being used for illustrative purposes only.*

Certain stock imagery © Thinkstock.

ISBN: 978-1-4759-6225-3 (hc)
ISBN: 978-1-4759-6223-9 (sc)
ISBN: 978-1-4759-6224-6 (eb)

Printed in the United States of America

iUniverse rev. date: 11/12/2012

Dedicated to
my perfectly dysfunctional family

Special thanks to

Allan Rust
Anson Mount
Jon Morris
Erin Granahan
Jeff Carlson
Erika Zuelke
Kelly Requa

My apologies to

The city of Fargo

CONTENTS

HOME
Cock-a-Doodle-Doo!

Fargo—where a day seems like a week, a week like a year, and a bullet to the head like a blessing. When I speak of Fargo, I technically speak of West Fargo, the smallest of the three sections—North Fargo and South Fargo being the other two. The last time I looked, the population was twelve thousand. It will either grow or be swallowed by weeds; neither would surprise me.

The city sits on the eastern border of North Dakota—so far east, in fact, there was apparently no room for an East Fargo. Our state is bordered by Minnesota, South Dakota, Montana, and the country of Canada. For those of you not familiar with North Dakota's terrain, it's ... how do I put this delicately? ... it has none. It's a huge football field full of wheat, with nothing taller than a cow to obstruct the horizon. If you suddenly drive off the road in a blizzard, you'll never know it. That's why we have fences around our fields: not to keep the cattle in, but to keep the cars out. Otherwise, who knows where you'd end up? "Oh my God, we're in Canada!"

North Dakota has been nicknamed the "Prairie State," and all one has to do is look out a window to realize that it's not an excessively imaginative title. But then, we're not overly imaginative people. The stark prairie terrain, as it washes over the edge of the North Dakota horizon, lends a feeling of infinite bland. Some say you can stand on the western border and wave to a friend on the eastern border. But the ones who say that are usually loaded on strawberry Boone's Farm. Aside from the definitive laws of physics, I guess the only obstacle that might block your view of the eastern border is Salem Sue, the world's largest statue of a Holstein cow.

Just outside of New Salem, it stands thirty-eight feet tall, fifty feet long, constructed entirely out of fiberglass and hollow—much like its entertainment value. It was built in Wisconsin for the New Salem Lions Club, and then transported in three parts. A professional artist was hired to direct the assembling. (Note: It's money well spent to have professional direction when putting three pieces of a cow together. A rank amateur might have made the embarrassing mistake of putting the head where the ass is supposed to be.) A website honoring the statue claims: "Salem Sue is known worldwide." Interesting. I defy you to travel anywhere outside of the tri-state area, much less the country, and find anyone who's heard of Salem Sue. Of course, I've never been to Zimbabwe. Maybe she's the talk of the town over there.

Despite possessing a glob of fiberglass in the shape of a cow, tourism has never been a strong point for us. State government recently suggested that the word *North* in our state's name is what's killing the tourist trade. But when all you've got to offer vacationers is a large cow statue, maybe the word *North* isn't your biggest problem. Adding insult to injury, in 1927 the folks in South Dakota chiseled away at a mountain until four presidents' faces were perfectly dimensioned in stone, right down to the pores in their skin. Washington, Jefferson, Teddy Roosevelt, and Lincoln all look down from their rocky mountaintop, reminding everyone that even the impossible is possible. After all that hard work, it's a real shame that Mount Rushmore doesn't have the worldwide popularity of Salem Sue.

The portrait of Fargo is similar to that of other older, medium-sized Midwestern towns: a main street, an elementary school and a high school, a library, and various businesses sprinkled throughout the remainder of the city. The city is bordered by the Red River on the east and the Sheyenne River on the west—each a branch of the mighty Mississippi, and each making flood disasters a way of life for the people of Fargo.

Traffic flow is meager enough to be managed with stop signs rather than stoplights. Because of one stubborn farmer, an odd few acres along Twelfth Street are still functioning as a grain field. He's holding out for the big bucks, and nobody's happy about it; after all, Fargo is a city on the make. Every entrepreneur in town has his eye on the plot of land. At one time Erv Raymond wanted to build a new bowling alley there; the Catholics believe another church should go up and are kneeling at attention with shovels in hand; and the Lutherans would like to build as well, but they're ... Lutherans, so they're about nine thousand bake sales short of an opening bid. Despite the haystacks, Twelfth Street has become one of the "hot spots." There is a row of new houses, a strip mall, and a Live Bait & Liquor store. It's a bewildering phenomenon to me that in order to own a store in the Midwest, it seems you're required to hand paint a sign that reads: Live Bait & ... [*fill in the blank*]. Night Crawlers & Beer. Minnows & Marshmallows. The second part doesn't matter. They're convinced that anything will sell better if advertised next to something that will help you catch fish. Leeches & Bibles.

Today I will be moving away from my hometown of twenty-three years, headed to Los Angeles, the land of hopes, dreams, and loose women with huge jugs. The truth behind my leaving is simple: I want more than what Fargo has to offer. I'm a dreamer, an artist; the passion to become the next big movie star is bursting from my pores. The television and movies were what honed my dreams from being an artist of some type to becoming an actor, and finally to the laser-sharp aspiration of being in *People* magazine.

Because of Fargo's modest disposition, I spent most of my childhood keeping my dreams to myself for fear of ... well, for fear of people saying, "Keep your dreams to yourself." The people of Fargo—in my eyes, anyway—have always seemed to believe less is more; I've always thought more will never be enough. Every week my mother was satisfied with simply reading *People* magazine, but not me, no sir. The only thing that would satisfy me was my face on the cover. And not a "body shot," mind you. I envisioned nothing less than bottom of my chin to the top of my hair covering the entire page. Comparatively, Fargonians have very, very, very subtle aspirations. They're content being content. They live in everydayness. They don't want to rock the boat; they want only to sit in it and troll around the lake on weekends. They want only to attend their afternoon card parties, with whist on Saturdays and pinochle on Sundays. They want for their weeknight bowling league to improve just a little each year, and maybe one day take that first place trophy, but only if it's in God's great plan. They have wants, yes, but no demands. They want their rainbow sherbet, but if lime sherbet is brought to the table, no one is going to jump up on a chair and yell, "I demand my rainbow sherbet. I've earned it. I've ordered it! *I want it!*" They sit there politely and profess the virtues of lime sherbet.

"Scottie, it's time," my mother yodels up the steps as if I'm still nine years old, which was my age when we first moved into our modest two-bedroom condo. "Rise and shine! Cock-a-doodle-doo!"

Because of her unique insanity, my mother is an endearing woman, and the only thing that gets in the way of our relationship is that she is my mother. If she were anyone else's mother, I could see myself being good friends with her. Even so, she has been the single constant in my life, the only person I could definitively count on when I was growing up. After divorcing my father and moving my brother Todd and me into our new home, she started working long, hard hours as a waitress at the local diner to make ends meet. With the exception of being on her feet all day, I think she loves working at a restaurant, especially the social aspect of it. She's the ultimate busybody. Other people's business fuels her.

Unfortunately, remembering names is not her strong point, so occasionally she'll associate regular customers with what meals they order on a regular basis. I imagine it's all the more jarring for victims when she applies the food-memory device outside the walls of the restaurant. Without any pretense, she'll walk up to someone in the grocery store; point a finger and say, "Eggs Benedict." Then, as if she had just called him by name, "How's your son doing in school?"

The terribly confused father squints and replies, "Which son?"

"The one that puts Tabasco sauce all over his fries?"

In harsh contrast, I myself will exert an alarming amount of energy in dodging people if I don't know their names. My mom, on the other hand, will proudly yell down a crowded Kmart aisle, "Western cheeseburger! Did you pass your kidney stone yet?"

It's this endearing lunacy that makes you want to call her Mom, even if she isn't yours. Everyone loves her. My friends like her because she makes the grilled cheese deluxe—which is basically a grilled cheese sandwich with a slice of bologna. She helps keep Gary, the Amway rep, in business; a smile on Mary Kay's face; and the cupboards full of Girl Scout cookies.

Physically, she is slender, with a gaunt face, which is exaggerated by the oversized white-framed glasses she wears. Her hair is continually permed, and each morning she brushes it in a manner that transforms the curls into waves that reach high into the air. The higher they reach, the better her mood. Before one perm has run its course, she'll start up another. If you look closely, you can see remnants of a perm from the seventies.

"I laid some sweatpants out for you on the toilet tank. Thought you might be more comfortable travelin' in those," she yells up the steps. I am surprised at the strength in her voice, as I know losing her first-born son to the world is going to hit hard as soon as I drive away.

Six in the morning feels like six in the morning no matter how exciting or important the event is I'm getting up for, which is why I set the alarm for eight. Today is the first day of the rest of my life outside the confines of repression, mind-numbing terrain, and Salem Sue, so I figured it was best not to go into it drowsy.

Out my bedroom window, I can see the day is gloomy and afflicted with gray. Through the haziness of the morning, I can still see the lone water tower, which after years of erosion has lost its *s* and now reads "We t Fargo." Trees line all the twelve streets and twelve avenues, forming a perfect grid-like forest. The low-hanging clouds are filled with a suspicion of rain, as if the weather is sad to see me go. I am sad as well, because I know moving to Los Angeles means I will never see weather again. Even our local meteorologist has given up on referring to the state of California. For him, California is no longer a place for weather; it's merely the portion of the map he stands in front of to deliver the national forecast. Occasionally, a New York cold front will cause him to lean eastward, revealing the states of Washington and Oregon. Every now and then something severe will pass over the Rockies, and he's forced to step back, thereby revealing the red-hot letters printed across the state of California: "Same old same old."

I won't, however, miss the winter blizzards the prairie can kick up. Nor will I miss having to go out into twenty-below temperatures at three in the morning because I forgot to plug in my car. That's right. You see, cars in the Midwest have a block heater that needs to be plugged in nightly to keep the engine warm. Often we string a big orange extension cord from the house to the plug, which dangles through the front of the grill.

My uncle Dwight is slightly simple—and when I say "slightly simple," I don't mean to suggest anything other than that he was from the South. Uncle Dwight, who moved back to Fargo with his family after having spent the first thirty years of his life bouncing around from one southern trailer park to the next, took one look at the cord dangling from the front of my car and asked, "Is that one of them there electric guitars?"

He meant "car" but said "guitar" simply because his brain felt more familiar with the phrase "electric guitar" and so it instructed his mouth to say it. After a while you learn to work the translations out on your own.

Not until this particular morning did I notice how perfectly my bedroom is lit at eight in the morning: not too bright, and yet bright enough for the airplanes to dive and swoop their way through the skyline-like wallpaper. Even though they're World War II fighter planes, I suppose it's childish not to have given them up to an adult coat or two of eggshell-white interior latex. Perhaps it was something my father would have done on a lazy weekend afternoon if he had been around. Perhaps.

My parents divorced years before divorce became fashionable. In fact, it was embarrassing. Many events in my life have been so affecting that in the middle of them, time appeared to suspend, thereby embedding every sight and sound into my memory for life. I was ten years old when the first happening of this type occurred.

I remember I was wearing my red scarf but had forgotten my mittens. As I grabbed the silver car-door handle, which was covered in a thick coating of frost, I jerked my hand back in shock. The chrome was so bone-chilling cold to the touch that I had to use a piece of my scarf to push in the knob of the handle, and my foot to pull open the door. As I climbed onto the seat, I considered it a little victory that I was getting away with not having to take my gloves to school.

That morning it was my mother's turn in the carpool rotation. As the sixth kid piled in, my heart stopped when he asked, "Why doesn't your dad drive anymore?" My victory with the gloves was instantly stripped of importance. In that fraction of a moment, my mind captured a picture. A soft lens filtered the images of all the kids in the car: of Brad, with his baseball cap that he wore defiantly under a winter stocking cap; of Mike, missing his two front teeth that had been knocked out that weekend; of Tyler, my best friend, who sat perfectly still in the middle of the front seat, kicking nervously at the bottom of the ashtray with his boot-covered toes. But the most vivid image was of my mother, who wore a purple turtleneck and had a tuft of her hair twirled up and cinched with a bobby pin.

I can still smell the car's musty upholstery. I could describe in detail the frost patterns on the windows, formed by my mother's haphazard scraping, which resulted in random diffusion of the sunlight as it landed on the kids' faces. To the boys, nothing was out of the ordinary; Glen had asked the question casually and in complete innocence.

So Glen, who was sitting directly behind me and thus hidden by the headrest, asked again, "When do you think your father will drive next?"

I could feel the blood pounding through my head as I wondered if I would have to answer the question. Or would it somehow be okay to just be silent? *Bang!* Another prodding kick to the back of my seat as Glen waited impatiently for an answer. He earnestly wanted to know when my father was going to be driving next, because everyone enjoyed his sense of humor.

My father made the trip to school less painful, I guess. He was a child of sorts himself and could easily strike our funny bone. His jokes were juvenile. On many occasions he would look out the side window and say, "Would you look at that!" After our attention was averted, he would hit the car horn and pump the brakes yelling, "Look out!" We screamed in fear of an accident, and as soon as we discovered it was a joke, we laughed like it was going out of style and punched at his shoulder. At stoplights he would pretend to fall asleep and start snoring as loud as he could. Once the light turned green and cars behind him started honking their horn, we would squeal with laughter and shake him awake. Our exaggerated reaction to his hijinks made my father pound on the steering wheel with delight.

I had a father that everyone loved and a mother that everyone loved; yet for some bewildering reason they didn't love each other. I couldn't figure out how that was possible and therefore concluded I must be part of the reason. Even kids who didn't carpool with us heard stories of my father's tomfoolery and were instantly filled with envy. For the most part, I was a very average student—not too smart, not too athletic, and with no special gifts—so in many ways the joy my father brought to the other kids is what defined me, which made it all the more important for me to conceal the divorce. I didn't want them to assume he was flawed.

And it wasn't until Glen posed that question that I fully understood: my father wasn't ever going to drive us again. I can still see their breath hanging in the air, the sun refracting off the frost, Mike's broken smile beaming, Tyler's toes tapping, and my mother's brown bobby pin. It was all there. I didn't want to be the one to tell them the news; so as the car zoomed down the street, I grabbed the door handle and yanked it open. *Screeech!* Mom hit the brakes, and the car swerved toward the curb as a cheer of delight from the kids in the back poured out the open door, along with their concerns for my father's absence. It proved to be the first in a lifelong cycle of deliberate diversions to avoid the subject of my parents' divorce. Indescribably difficult effort would go into dodging the topic. The emotional pain of simply admitting that my father no longer lived with us would have been a tea party in comparison to the pain and labor that went into covering it up.

By the age of thirteen, I was an expert at coming up with excuses for my father's absence: "He's out of town a lot." "Ahh, he came down with a case of … Schlitz." "I'm sorry, he can't make the father-son trivia competition, but this is my uncle Dwight. He's harmless." My efforts were probably in vain, as the town was small enough for news like that to spread fast. But perhaps out of sympathy, the townspeople would pretend not to know, which made me feel better.

Like all midwesterners, I became good at doing the dance of dodging emotions and stuffing painful feelings deep down inside so I didn't have to experience them. Out of sight, out of mind. Strangely enough, we've even conditioned ourselves to keep feelings of joy in check. It's okay to be happy, but to express it would somehow be rude. It's gloating, and God may punish you. Just ride it out for five minutes and hopefully the euphoria will pass. But one mustn't forget that bubbling under all this repressed emotion lives a volcanic Tony Soprano. Inside every midwesterner is an episode of *The Sopranos* disguised as an episode of *Leave It to Beaver*. Even Mom's got a little Tony in her, but it's all subtext.

What she says is this: "Scott, Todd, those cookies are for church, so don't touch 'em, please."

What she means is this: "Listen up, cocksuckers, those goddamn cookies are for church. Don't touch 'em or I'll cut your fuckin' fingers off and shove 'em so far up your ass you'll be picking your nose."

If acid isn't constantly eating away at our Midwestern stomach lining, we're not content.

My journey begins as I climb into my rusted-out, faded blue Dodge Dart, which makes it look less like I'm going to conquer the big, cruel world and more like I'm off to tackle a scarf at a knitting bee. The rain is coming down hard, yet I am not at all surprised to see that half of the yards I pass still have their sprinklers going. I think to myself, "That's why I have to leave. I want to be from a town where I find that peculiar."

I turn right down Sheyenne Street, which will lead me through the heart of town to the highway. Sheyenne is the main drag, the bread and butter of our streets. It is named for the Sheyenne River, which runs parallel. Sheyenne is not to be confused with the Cheyenne Indian tribe; or maybe it is, and the people who named the river just spelled it wrong. I mean it's not a stretch to believe it was a spelling error. After all, the state was established by Norwegians and Polish.

The stretch of road that lay before me represents the twelve blocks of my childhood. At a time like that, you secretly hope the town has gathered together in the wee hours to plan a spectacular ticker tape farewell for you. And as you drive by the rows of people who have lined the streets to wave good-bye, you can see tears in the women's eyes; the veterans are poised in a military salute; the flag at the post office is at half mast; and all the kids are cheering you, because a day of school was cancelled for your departure. And perhaps the young, good-looking college girls, so overwhelmed with grief, would flash me their breasts. But from what I can see, perched at the only stoplight in town, the streets are empty, the classrooms are full, including the bras, and the little storefronts are busy going on with their business.

TWELFTH STREET
Transsexual or Wannabe?

Nearly every car radio in Fargo is tuned to AM 790, and mine is no exception. After listening to a few minutes of the *Farmers Market* radio show, an out-of-towner might assume the radio is *stuck* on AM 790 and feel sorry for the poor sap whose car it is. The secret behind the success of the *Farmers Market* is that it has the same hypnotic effect as a television infomercial; both are train wrecks that you can never seem to turn off. It's on in full force as I turn into the Stop & Shop to load up on Mountain Dew, sunflower seeds, and some pink Sno Balls for the long trip.

HOST: Good morning, you're on with the *Farmers Market* radio rhow, coming to you out of Fargo, North Dakota. We've had a busy morning on the *Farmers Market*: sold George Haberman's fiberglass garage door to a Cass County man, and just past the hour we sold Bert Tollerud's rototiller. But we have time for just a few more callers.

MYRTLE (fragile, older): Yes, this is Myrtle Haberman. I'm looking to see if anyone has some extra rhubarb?

HOST: You need some rhubarb? What are ya gonna to be makin', some pies, then?

MYRTLE: Yeah, pies and bars.

HOST: Mmmm, those rhubarb bars are tasty.

MYRTLE: Yeah, they sure are.

HOST: Well, we'll put out the word and try to track ya down some rhubarb.

MYRTLE: Okie-dokie, thank you.

HOST: Hello, you're on with the *Farmers Market*.

HANK: Yeah, this is Hank, I just wanted to thank you for helping get my manure spreader sold.

HOST: Oh, when did it sell?

HANK: Same day. Guy calls up and says he heard on the *Farmers Market* that I got my spreader for sale. Then he says he'll be right over and git it.

HOST: That's a heck of a deal.

HANK: You said it. Now I'm hoping you can help sell an auger I got laying around.

HOST: Oh, you got an extra auger, huh?

HANK: Yeah, she's a dandy. Little old, but a fella could clean her up.

HOST: What are you askin' for her?

HANK: Three hundred.

HOST: Oh, that's a heck of a deal.

HANK: Not too bad. They can call me at 282-4919. Just ask for Hank, I'll be sittin' around here all day.

HOST: Do you happen to have any rhubarb lying around, Hank?

HANK: No, I don't. Sorry.

HOST: Okay, very good. Good luck then with that auger.

All four of Stop & Shop's parking spots are empty, so I pull into the one just outside the front door. Janet Johnson has worked here since I was a child and waves as I make my way past the four aisles, which include candy, snacks, canned goods, and housewares, to the back wall of coolers. Janet was the only person I knew who never made eye contact—ever.

Shortly after moving to Florida, her daughter, Jennifer, committed suicide by slicing open her arm. I learned in junior high that with blood comes respect—unless it's the product of a suicide, and then the blood only carries shame. It's this shame that Janet the Stop & Shop cashier has been carrying around for twelve years. I never knew her daughter directly because she was eight years older than me, but what fascinated me about her, even more than the suicide, was the fact that she was the only person I knew who had moved out of the state of North Dakota.

The summer before going into the seventh grade, Mom came home from work one day with the news about Jennifer and confused me in a way only she can into remembering it. Like a juggler, she is capable of layering three or four subjects into one conversation. After she's done, you can, surprisingly, remember everything, even though at the time it was spewing out of her mouth, you didn't understand a single word. Her relentless stream of consciousness is sort of numbing and puts you in a conversational coma.

"Oh gosh, I almost forgot; evidently there's been an incident with Janet's daughter," Mom said while whipping me up a sandwich.

"Who's Janet?" I asked.

"Johnson. Janet Johnson, the one who works at the Stop & Shop but used to work at OK Hardware. Of course, that was when you were very small, you wouldn't—is it Jennifer or Jackie? I do know she took her baby and moved to Florida after high school. Oh, I can't keep it straight with these hot flashes. That new medication Dr. Strand prescribed makes me loopy, and I can't remember a—Jennifer, that's right, just like Larry's daughter. Anyway, apparently—do you want fries with this? Oh, what am I thinking? The FryDaddy's on the fritz; it's in the shop, two weeks now. I'm just sick about it. She's in the hospital: dead, or maybe she's alive. I couldn't get the details straight. We were so busy today; there's that John Deere convention in South Fargo, what a mess; but if she is alive—it doesn't look hopeful. I'm surprised I didn't know sooner, since Janice is Janet's neighbor and comes into the restaurant pert-near every day. You know Janice; she's the one that always orders the Cobb salad—morning, noon, or night, Cobb salad. She's crazy, you know, always going on about car trouble or teeth problems; she's not happy with that new dentist, Linderman. Well, I've heard not many are, what with charging an arm and a leg just to sit you in the chair. I don't know who he thinks he is—some 'fan-dangled' dentist from Minneapolis, I imagine. So yeah, sliced her arm with a razor blade, I guess. You'll want to make sure you don't mention it to Janet when you're in the Stop & Shop, then."

I never said a word about the suicide to Janet, but it was the only thing I ever thought about when Mom sent me down to the store with a list of items that included razor blades. I was petrified setting them down on the counter, thinking the wrong amount of smile might trigger horrifying memories.

"So you're leavin' us, huh? For how long?" she asks as I carefully place my items on the counter.

"For good. Or until I run out of money, which might be Seattle," I joke, hoping a little fun wouldn't trigger horrifying memories.

"I thought you were going to California?"

"I am."

"Soooo …?"

"Seattle is on the way."

"Well, I don't know anything about that, but I sure know we're gonna miss ya."

"Ahh, thanks."

She fumbles with the package of Sno Balls, rolling them over in her hand, searching for the bar code, and then stops. She taps out the numbers directly on the register and stops again. She stares at the pack as if she doesn't know what to do next. The shop is so silent I can hear the hum of the refrigerator motors. What had I triggered?

"These were my daughter's favorite," she says.

Damn. "Yes, well … I've been known to be girlie," I say, trying to invert the heavy energy.

She lifts her head from the Sno Balls, and for the first time looks straight at me; and I notice a sweetness radiating from her beautiful, tranquil blue eyes, framed evenly by premature wrinkles. No words from either of us, but I give every effort to radiate sympathy. From deep in the fiber of my emotions, a certain compassion for her daughter is surfacing from the knowledge that, like me, she also made the choice to leave home.

Janet breaks through the sound of the refrigerator with "She left the nest, too. After high school she moved with her baby's daddy to

Florida. *Her* daughter's called Jennifer too, but we call her Jenny so there's no ... no confusion."

"Sure." I keep my answers brief as Mom's warning echoes in my head.

"She lives with Dad. Yeah, he's a nice boy, but they're in Florida, so we don't see them much. Pictures, you know. That kind of thing."

There is something powerful in both leaving and being left. Perhaps knowing she may never see me in the Stop & Shop again gives Janet the courage to broach the subject. Standing there with keys in my hand and Los Angeles as my destination, I realize I no longer answer to my mom. If I feel compelled to engage in conversation about her daughter, then I can.

"I'm sorry about your daughter."

She smiles briefly, and her eyes avert back to the Sno Balls as she places the items into a bag. "Anything else for ya then?"

The front door swings open, and the bell clangs against the glass. Burt from the bakery walks in and grabs the paper. "Mornin', Janet."

Janet turns her head and smiles at him. "How's it goin', Burt?"

Burt's morning ritual of grabbing the paper, placing his two quarters on top of the register, and walking out is halted by her use of eye contact. He stops, turns to me, and looks back at Janet and smiles. "Dandy."

"Good deal."

"Mornin', Scott."

"Morning."

"Headed out today?"

"Yep."

"Knock 'em dead out there," he says with a pat on my shoulder. "Say, listen, make sure ya git your petro in Jamestown. I heard Bismark's fuel is pretty pricey."

"Will do."

"Alrighty then, have a safe trip, and, Janet, you stay out of trouble. Toodleoo."

Janet and I wave, which is awkward because I'm standing with my bag in hand, ready to walk out as well. But I imagine it is awkward only for me, as most North Dakotans are accustomed to very long good-byes. Often a good-bye can last for hours while people stand next to their car with keys in hand and summarize the last two hours of their life.

"Okay, well, I should hit the road."

"Okie-dokie. Well, have a safe trip then," she says in a nurturing quality.

"Will do."

Every day on a bench, under the protection of the Stop & Shop's awning, you can find Roy Byer, the town fortune-teller, as he likes to refer to himself. He used to be the janitor at the high school and moved in a manner that suggested his hip flexor might give out whenever he took a step. This made his dust mop control a little questionable; nevertheless, Roy the hip-challenged janitor had the job of sweeping the court at halftime of every basketball game.

Nowadays, Roy sits out front and tells your future by way of *Farmers Almanac* and an old Texas Instruments calculator. The poor hip is not his only ailment; he's also afflicted with a harelip, which makes it nearly impossible to understand a word of your future.

"Hey, Thot," Roy mumbles as I open my car door. "I muth whon you. Me carehul on hersday if uh hurd hies over your hehicle you will me thide thwiped by uh themi. Tho watch out!"

"Thanks, buddy. You too."

You only ever hear enough to know your life is in danger, but never enough to prevent disaster from happening; and evidently everyone future in Fargo is in peril.

Roy has been outside the store every day, save for winters, for the last two years, except for the time he volunteered his talents to Daniel Sonnenberg's bake sale; Daniel was raising money for a sex change operation. He is the son of Revered Sonnenberg, the local Lutheran minister. Trying to maintain the integrity of the Lutheran church—whose ideologies are about as inspirational as a recipe for potato chip casserole—must be difficult enough without your son deciding one day that he wants to become a woman. The Lutherans, a minority organization, already had a questionable reputation in the religious community, and this was certainly going to damage them further. To make things worse, on the outside wall of the sanctuary, some hoodlum spray-painted "Catholicism for salvation, Lutheranism for beauty tips."

I understood Daniel's feelings of being trapped and wanting something that was presently out of reach. Daniel's one desire in life was to become a woman. Living in Fargo and being raised by a minister was the least conducive environment in the world for this to happen—far more challenging than becoming a celebrity. Daniel was two years ahead of me in high school, but we shared the same homeroom. As evidenced by Daniel's actions, his game plan was to become the best son possible, earnestly hoping his father would then grant him the approval for a sex change. He was a straight-A student who participated in the speech club, debate team, chess club, jazz choir, and band, and he wrote for the school paper and was president of the student council. That is the agenda of a boy who is trying to make himself look good in the eyes of his father and, in turn, his father look good in the eyes of God. But it was all for naught. After twenty years of failing to please his father, he finally imploded and thought, "Fuck it! I'm chopping off my dick!"

Daniel's announcement put his father in the hospital and left the congregation with a senile replacement from Litchfield, who from time to time would ask the congregation to open their Bibles to the book of Kenny. In all fairness, it turned out his new great-grandson was named Kenny.

Daniel was about ten thousand dollars short of a vagina, which is really what sets apart transsexuals from wannabes. So he decided to spearhead a bake sale for his "cause." But asking the good people of Fargo to buy a lemon bar or a brownie to help fund an operation that would construct a vagina out of a penis was going to be trickier than backing a boat trailer into a lake after consuming a twelve-pack of Bud. I don't know how much money Daniel ended up making, but apparently it wasn't enough, as he continued his bake sales out of town for the bulk of the summer. But finally, after a three-state tour of the "I Will Be Woman, Hear Me Roar" bake sale, he reached his financial goal. I think the bulk of the donations came from the people of Minneapolis, who are more liberal with sexuality.

Daniel was a tall, gangly, unattractive man, and after the operation became Denise, a tall, gangly, unattractive woman. There is only so much a long wig and makeup can do for a man who could pass as Herman Munster. But Denise seemed much happier than Daniel ever did, and in the end, that's what matters. As for the community of Fargo, they took the comfortable middle road, neither embarrassing her nor dismissing her; yet the majority of them continued to call her Daniel. But one day, a few winters later, after a church service, I overheard an elderly woman say, "Denise, could you help me with my jacket?" I remember smiling and thinking to myself, *There's hope.*

As I hop back into my car in the Stop & Shop parking lot, I wonder if on a certain level, conscious or unconscious, Daniel's bold move to swap genders is what prodded my decision to leave home.

While pulling out and taking a left onto Sheyenne Street, the *Farmers Market* show is just wrapping up.

HOST: Where you callin' from, Clarence?

CLARENCE: Peemer.

HOST: Peemer?

CLARENCE: Yeah, Peemer.

HOST: Very good, then. So listen, Myrtle's out in Yanktown, just a couple miles north of Peemer.

CLARENCE: Oh yeah?

HOST: Yeah.

CLARENCE: Good.

HOST: Yeah. So, Myrtle, if you're still listening, Hank can hook you up with some rhubarb in Peemer. Which ain't too far. That should pert-near be a straight shot from where you are, I'd think. So just give Hank a call at—Hank what's your number out there in Peemer? Hank? … Okie-dokie, we lost Hank. Well, Myrtle, you just head south on Highway 6 till you hit Peemer and someone there should know where Hank the rhubarb guy lives.

ELEVENTH STREET
Flipper Tooth

From my passenger window I can see South Elementary, which sits on the northwest corner of Eleventh Street. An L-shaped, one-story brick structure lined with split-pea-green tile. It's there that my official school life began and ran through West Fargo High School. One of the few remaining phone booths in the city lives just outside the Stop & Shop, which is kitty-corner from the school. Since my elementary school days were filled with humiliation, ridicule, and beatings, it was always comforting to know that my mom was just a phone call away. It was never more comforting than when I was being chased by the school bully or losing feeling in my limbs from the dead of winter. Both were equally brutal, and over the years, each took a toll on my body.

Terry Rolson had a wicked uppercut, and December a mean cold front. But there was never a pile of presents at the end of Terry. He was gloomy through and through. Terry was not only a bully, but also my next-door neighbor. He always claimed he held two black belts in karate. Whenever anyone asked him what the other one was for he always replied, "Karate, dipshit." Terry had a scar on his upper lip and sandy brown hair that resembled a heap of Pick Up Stix.

One wintry recess Terry grabbed my hands and spun me in a circle until I slipped out of my gloves and went flying face-first into a tetherball pole. Little did I know at the time: Terry actually changed my life for the better.

Upon regaining consciousness, I was lying on a cot in the nurse's room with a bloody T-shirt and bitter residue in the back of my throat. I was told that I lost my right front tooth, and it would be replaced with a denture piece that I could take out at will—a "flipper" they called it. Flipper was my new best friend, and by the end of the year, I had learned to do tricks with it. Without the use of my hands, I could remove it from my mouth, and with the assistance of my tongue, deftly place it on the bridge of my nose. As far as maneuvers went, it was brilliant. The most productive aspect of the trick was that it brought me something I had hitherto not acquired: the attention of the popular kids. This began my foray into becoming one of the envied in life, at least by fourth-graders. Denture tricks had became my own little way to win friends and influence people. And a bully named Terry made it all happen.

My fame spread quickly, throughout not just the school, but the entire district. By the sixth grade I was known regionally as Flipper. While shopping at the mall with Mom, students from neighboring schools would ask me if I was the tooth guy.

"Flipper," I was quick to correct. And if I determined they weren't one of the elite in their school district, I would use my haughty tone to put them in their place.

"Flipper, right. Hey, Flip," they would ask, automatically shortening my nickname because they felt an immediate connection. "Can you do that nose trick?"

I would roll my eyes in exasperation hoping to communicate that I had been fielding that request all day long and was nearly at the end of my emotional and physical rope. After sufficiently ridiculing their uninspired request to the point of public humiliation, I would proceed to balance my plastic tooth on my nose.

Another popular stunt was to spit it five inches straight into the air and catch it in my mouth like a grape—absolutely amazing to witness ... when it worked. The problem with this trick was the lack of consistency in my ability to catch it. When I didn't catch it, the flipper would land on the floor, usually slide under a desk, and tumble through a pile of dust bunnies. Amusing, but not the desired outcome.

Because of the gluttonous nature of our society, my classmates quickly became disenchanted with the five inches and began pushing me to spit it higher. I managed to launch it three feet once, but it came down with such force that it lodged in the back of my throat. At the time, the school nurse was at lunch, so the woodshop teacher had to remove it with a pair of needle-nose pliers.

I spent hours at home developing new tricks out of fear of losing my popularity. I even indulged other students in any lame tricks they would devise. My tooth served as a hacky sack and as a puck for table hockey, and we once even attached to a paper airplane. Brad Teller, the other bully, had the idea to pretend to punch me in the face while I simultaneously bit down on a ketchup packet to create the illusion that he had knocked out my tooth. I'm not sure who Brad thought he would be fooling, since the seventy-five kids in our elementary school all knew I had a fake tooth, but this didn't stop his weekly request.

A popular trick among the demented lunch students involved me launching my denture into an unsuspecting peer's bowl of tomato soup when he looked away. We would all sit back with great anticipation until the poor kid pulled up a spoonful of Flipper.

I was gaining friends exponentially. Everyone wanted to hang out with me. It was my first taste of celebrity and consequently created a growing hunger in me for public attention—a hunger that was not easily satisfied in a state where the primary vocation was growing barley.

Once I reached junior high, my popularity worked against my desire for mass attention, as the jocks all wanted me to join the football team and the basketball team and any other team that involved group sweating. I wasn't good at sweating. Despite my lack of athletic agility, I hung in and stayed the course until sophomore year, when I broke my leg for the second time. The first was on the eighth-grade football team when I stepped in a gopher hole. The second was on the JV basketball team when I tripped on the mascot after missing a breakaway layup. At that point I determined it was time for a new extracurricular activity. I made a bold move that would put me in jeopardy of losing every ounce of popularity I had acquired over the previous six years.

My friend Tyler was trying out for the fall musical *Annie Get Your Gun* and wanted me to audition for a small, nonsinging part. The auditions were held after school in the auditorium. About forty students showed up, cackling and laughing like they were apart of some secret actors' society, that I was not readily going to be invited into. For half an hour I sat in an orange, hard-plastic theatre seat and watched student after student read effortlessly from the script they had apparently been given before the audition.

Finally, Tyler elbowed me to go up after the director yelled, "We need a male up there!" As I walked up the stairs to the stage, someone handed me a book and pointed to a part that was apparently an Indian chief. The only thing I knew about how an Indian would sound or act was from my grandpa, who used to impersonate one while telling his favorite joke. The first line in the script was "I squeeze your neck till your eyes pop out of your head like grapes." The Indian in my grandpa's joke was drunk, and stumbled about slurring his words, so that's exactly what I did while reading my lines. The society of actors looking up at me from their orange seats immediately started laughing, which I interpreted to mean failure.

"Keep going!" the director yelled from the back row, which led me to believe I was actually making them laugh as a result of my performance. It was exhilarating.

Being on stage for those ten minutes during the audition was more thrilling than the hours of adulation I had received from my denture tricks. A whole new level of desire for celebrity was created in me. Filled with excitement and satisfaction, I ran the entire way home that night. I couldn't sleep; all I could do was recite the line over and over again to the ceiling, "I squeeze your neck till your eyes pop out of your head like grapes." *Maybe I should have said it louder or faster*, I thought. I tossed and turned with regret upon each new way I could have delivered the lines. It was clear that sleep was not going to happen until the next day, when the cast list was posted.

Despite my ninety-eight-pound physique and pale Norwegian complexion, I landed the role of Sitting Bull: a two-hundred-pound, sunburned senior citizen. And just like that, I was officially a member of the Society of Actors, otherwise known to the rest of the high school population as Drama Fags. My days of being the cool guy with the fake tooth were over.

I remember getting my first laugh on opening night. I was center stage. The laughter rolled over me, and my instinct to hold for the laugh was innate. And in that three-second holding pattern, I thought to myself: *This is it. This is what I want to do with my life.*

I determined that nothing was going to stop me, not even my mother's inability to recognize my talent or provide normal, positive reinforcement.

"Scott, you looked spiffy up there. I loved them feathers. The feathers were the best part of the show for me." I'll never know why she always thought my costumes had something to do with me and not the designer. "Golly gee, they were pretty. I didn't realize you were so talented. How did you know how to make feathers?" She asked.

"I didn't," I said, completely dejected.

"Well then, that's even more amazing."

"No. Mom, I—I didn't make the feathers."

"Well, who on earth made the feathers then?"

I rolled my eyes in frustration. "I believe a bird made them."

What she said next was this: "Listen mister, there is no reason to get smart-mouthed with me. I just wanted to know who made the feathers."

What she meant was this: "Shut your fucking face before I staple it shut, you little bastard, and don't think I won't."

The other tactic she would employ to judge my performances hinged on whether or not she liked the character. If the character behaved in a courteous manner, then I performed well.

"Gee, that sure was nice work. You were so sweet up there. Why can't you be more like that at home?"

If the character was evil, then she would gingerly say, "Gee, you weren't very nice up there to that sweet girl. What was that all about? I don't know why you couldn't have treated her better."

"Neil Simon wanted it that way."

"What was that sweet girl's name up there anyhow?"

"Karen."

"Ooooooh, is that the Grindberg girl? I didn't recognize her. She's put on quite a lot of weight. You know, her father comes into the restaurant pert-near every day and orders the Reuben with extra sauerkraut. Gosh, she was sweet up there. I bet her parents are proud of her."

I certainly got my flare for drama from my mother. She's a big, Midwestern drama queen, and her dramas are played out in every second of life; whereas, I like to contain mine to the stage. Everything is dramatic with her, be it other people's marriages, death, or feathers. She can pull her head out of the fridge and with a tragic sigh say, "I just can't believe we're out of mayo already. I just don't know where it all goes." Or she'll yell, "Bingo!" like she just won the lottery and can finally retire.

I spent the next three years after the success of *Annie Get Your Gun* attempting to astonish the high school theatre community with dazzling character transformations such as Maurice in *Death of a Hired Hand*, where I played a black slave who was dying of old age, or Captain von Trapp in *The Sound of Music*.

Tyler and I even created a stage version of the film *Smokey and the Bandit*—minus the Trans Am. I wanted to use a car, but the school said the stage wouldn't hold the weight, so I used my mom's bike instead. A certain amount of *Bandit* style was lost on the pink basket, but I think my cowboy hat and western shirt offset it. I duct-taped a walkie-talkie to the handlebars that acted as my CB when I communicated with Snowman, played by Tyler, who was driving a ten-speed. On each side of the stage I built a ramp that led down into the audience, where we could loop around the lobby and come back up the other aisle. The production was brilliant despite the lack of turnout.

My artistic efforts went largely unappreciated in high school. The citizens of Fargo filled their cultural appetites at venues like the County Fair Variety Show, which was produced by the 4-H girls, and usually staged in a hog barn. How was I to compete with that? If art to you is a doll made from a corncob; pine cones glued to anything and spray-painted; or yarn knit into something with which you could grab a hot pot, then there is no way you're going to appreciate the subtle, psychological undertones that I layered into *Smokey and the Bandit*. If a soft piece of pine shaped into your favorite farm animal interests you, or you have an oversize wooden spoon and fork hanging on the wall in your kitchen, you're probably not going to come to a screeching stop when you drive past the high school marquee and see an advertisement for a theatrical version of *Smokey and the Bandit*. A bust of Shakespeare carved out of a cake of butter? Yes. But not original theatre.

As I make my final drive past the school today, I can't help but flinch at the thought of my first car ride past here when I was fourteen. Because I worked on my grandparents' farm, I was able to get my driver's license earlier than everyone else. So the first day behind the wheel I cruised past a group of girls on the junior high cheerleading squad, honked, and waved with pride, all cocky, like I was Elvis or something.

By the eighth grade, the novelty of my denture tricks had worn off, and I was left with nothing but two fake teeth. I was no longer someone you wanted to bring home to Mom. But on that day, I felt like I once again had something to offer, something to bring to the relationship table, even to a girl as important as a cheerleader. As I drove past, I casually rested my arm across the top of the seat and pointed my index finger at them while running my other hand through my hair, proving that not only could I drive, but I could also drive with no hands.

From my rearview mirror I saw them all laughing and pointing at me. "Of course they're pointing," I thought. "They're pointing at how cool I am." I was quickly securing an invite to the Sadie Hawkins dance in the spring. But sadly, they were laughing at what I saw from my rearview mirror. Trailing behind me was the fifty-foot, orange extension cord that I forgot to unplug before backing out of the driveway. Apparently the end that was attached to the outlet on the house released before the one on the front grill of my car. The cord was bouncing around like a towrope missing a fallen water-skier.

In *any* junior high, an act of that nature is so uncool, so un-Elvis-like, that nothing can erase it, not even being the only one able to drive to school. All it does is give everyone a year to mock you until they get their own licenses and no longer care. Dragging a fifty-foot, orange cord behind you for seventeen blocks sends out a clear message to young, hot, cheerleader types: *Hey, look at me, I'm an idiot. Whatever you do, do not invite me to the Sadie Hawkins dance. I'm cancer for your reputation.*

Events like this have stayed with me and haunted me for years. I can't seem to let go; in fact, I play them over and over in my head. On the day of my high school graduation I was still explaining to some of the girls: "My mom had forgotten to unplug the cord; it wasn't me," and they were like, "What cord? What are you talking about, freak?"

"You know, five years ago, the fifty-foot, orange cord that I was dragging behind my car?" I pleaded in desperation.

Michelle, the head cheerleader and prom queen, squinted a little as she tilted her head to one side. "Hey, can you still put your tooth on your nose?"

TENTH STREET
Whoops, Just Let a Boomer!

As I pull up to the Tenth Street stop sign, I can hear the creaking of the Pabst Blue Ribbon sign that swings from the window of the bowling alley. Erv Raymond owns the bowling alley, which sits on the east side of Sheyenne, just past Tenth Street. Of course, at eight thirty in the morning it's still closed. You can always tell when it's closed because Erv bars the door with a garden hoe for an extra level of security. But the garden hoe is not why it hasn't been broken into for twenty years. No, what discourages the thieves is the fact that it's a bowling alley, and there's a perfectly good bank across the street.

As I stop at the intersection, Allan Grossman makes his way down the middle of the street on his morning jog. Despite his last name, he's a good-looking guy, a cross between a disheveled Elvis and Robert Redford. After noticing me he runs across the street to my passenger window.

"How ya doin', Scott?" Allan is a mile from his home, yet not a drop of sweat can be found anywhere on him—which makes me wonder if he was actually jogging or just getting out of the house. He's two years older than me, and married his high school sweetheart immediately after graduation.

"Good. You?"

"Oh, you know, not too bad."

This conversation is happening right in the middle of the street because it can. In Fargo you just stop your car anytime, anywhere, for any reason, or no reason, and chances are a traffic jam will not ensue. Horns aren't used to prevent collisions; they're for getting someone's attention in order to wave at them.

"Good."

"Leavin'?"

"Yep, headed out of town as we speak."

There are people in this world who are better friends with you than you are with them. That's the case with Allan. He's one of those goofy guys that never fits in anywhere, but is nice enough that you just can't deny him attention. He would wear mismatched clothes that he purchased from the Salvation Army, not to save money, but rather as a failed attempt at being an individual. I remember one morning he showed up for class wearing a robe. The teacher asked him to take it off because it showed a "lack of respect for the institution."

"Are you sure you want me to take this off?"

"Yes, Allan."

Allan let the robe drop to the floor, and with a rocket-like reaction, the teacher demanded he put it back on.

Also, Allan lives with a secret—a really juicy secret—and every waking moment he suffers from the anxiety that it might somehow get out. A few years ago, his secret altered my perception of human sexuality.

For years my sex life had limped along at a very slow pace. Perhaps it was due to the odd sort of way it unfolded throughout my youth.

My foray into sex started innocently, and in the same way I assume it does with most other kids: by playing doctor. When we're very young there are no gender boundaries. The neighbor kids and I played doctor in our forts and basements with whoever was around at the time. One child took down his or her pants and another began an exploratory examination. No emotions. No complications. Just a bunch of teeny weenies and baby boobies.

At the age of twelve I cemented the first sexual landmark in my life when I took a passionate interest in ladies' bowling. That's when I turned my sexual interests toward humans. Two years prior, I had lost my virginity to my Winnie the Pooh bear, the one my grandma gave me for my fifth birthday. Those of you with weak stomachs might want to skip ahead to the next chapter.

Still reading? Consider yourself a pervert.

At age nine I had yet to discover masturbation, so most evenings I would rub my naked body against the mattress or grind my groin into the pillow. One night I noticed a small hole in the seam of Winnie's crotch, so I ripped open a slit, pulled out some stuffing, and the next thing I knew, Winnie and I were at Macy's picking out china patterns. It's as simple as that. It was addictive. I couldn't get enough Pooh-tang. And it seemed as though Winnie couldn't take his paws off me. We employed the missionary position most of the time, but occasionally Winnie would enjoy bouncing on top of me.

But sadly, like any relationship, it got complicated. There came a point when Winnie could no longer satisfy me. I struggled to achieve orgasm; in fact, I achieved more chafing than orgasm. Soon after, our affair ended and he moved on to the *National Counsel for Lutheran Women's Thrift Store.*

It filled my mother with pride when I attended her Thursday night bowling league. But I wasn't there out of admiration for my mom's talent; I showed up each week to see Jane Peterson's ass peek out from under her miniskirt every time she released the ball. The sight was heaven-sent. Jane was a thirty-five-year-old divorcee who wore a brown tweed skirt and silk panties, which by the middle of the third game, rode high into the luxurious crack of her ass and sent me racing into the men's room to unload my adolescent pressure cooker. I credit Jane for introducing me to masturbation—not formally, of course, but through her mere presence—and once locked safely in a stall I had nothing to rub against but my own hand.

Soon I equated bowling with sex, and by summer vacation all I could think about was bowling. Twice a day I desired to get my hands on some "bowling." Every hormone in my body pleaded with my mother until she finally agreed to pay my way through an eight-week professional bowling camp. As it turned out, bowling camp was no place to get laid. There were only two women at camp, and neither of them had the sex appeal of Jane. Neither one of them wore a tweed skirt that rode up to reveal her ass. I wound up sexually frustrated, but with significantly improved bowling skills. In time, I became the top bowler in my Saturday juniors league, three-time state juniors champion, and toyed with the idea of joining the pro circuit.

Once I got to high school I determined bowling was only going to get in the way of acquiring babes. Equally hindering, if not more, was living under the same roof as my mom. First off, Mom has gas—bad gas. And gas is not conducive to bringing over the ladies. Ron Popeil is her God: Veg-O-Matic, Mince-O-Matic, Dial-O-Matic—if it's "O-Matic," it's in her cupboard. Mom will buy anything off the television that fries food. But her pride and joy is the Fry Daddy. First it was the Fry Daddy Jr.; then when I was in high school she upgraded to the Fry Daddy Sr.—the Cadillac of Fry Daddys, which led to the Cadillac of gas. Even though the fryer was a staple in our family, it was the bane of her health problems.

"Oh gosh, I'm having a hot flash. Why do I keep having so many hot flashes?"

I shrug sarcastically, if that's possible, and say, "Well, perhaps it's from stooping over a vat of boiling lard all day."

Then, after dinner, "Uff dah, I'm bloated. It's that darn fried food. It's so good, but I get so darn bloated."

And "bloated" means she's minutes away from gassy, and I'm minutes away from nausea. But Mom doesn't fart, mind you; she lets "boomers." A *boomer* is her cute word for passing gas. We'll be walking through Kmart, Wal-Mart, any mart, pick a mart; she doesn't discriminate when it comes to flatulence. Suddenly I'll hear, *Phhtt!* And they're so loud that she is obligated to acknowledge them. "Whoops, I just let a boomer."

"Mom!"

"Oh, boomers don't smell. It's just air."

"Yeah, air that comes from your ass. And boomers can be heard."

"Keep your voice down, mister. Nobody needs to hear us talk about my boomers."

"But they've already heard the boomer," I would reply. "Our talking is not alerting them to something they don't already know."

Mom's nightly wandering minstrel show, too, made it awkward for any of my friends who were sleeping over. I have always been a "night owl," a phrase my mother uses to describe me to her friends, because apparently it's their business. Every single night I would stay up late, watching TV in the living room, and every night Mom would wake up around midnight, having been asleep for three hours, and make her way down the stairs to see what could possibly be going on—as if, after so many years, there might be someone else down on the couch, such as a cat burglar who had broken in to watch Letterman. She was always shocked to find me up and always asked what I was doing, and I would turn the TV down to answer, "Watching TV."

As if this madness wasn't exasperating enough, every night she slept in a ten-year-old cotton nightgown, which had worn a little too thin for my taste, and would shuffle down the stairs scratching her ass. The woman could not help but scratch her ass in the middle of the night. And you could hear it coming from the next county. *Scraaatch! Scraaatch!* It was a special treat when Tyler and I would invite a few freshman girls over on a weekend to see if we could parlay their ignorance of our geekiness into some sweet necking.

Scraaatch! Scraaatch!

"What's that?" a friend might ask after being startled. "Do you have wolves? Was that a wolf scratchin' at the door?"

In shame, I would have to admit, "Just my mom scratching her ass. Prep yourself. The show will be starting in exactly seven point five seconds."

Also, before going to bed, she would liberally apply Vaseline to her lips. Or Vicks; it didn't matter which. Even though it usually ended up all around the perimeter of her mouth, she'd apply a little in and around her nose in case it got dry in the night, and pretty much anywhere else, until her finger was empty. So as she made her way down the steps in the dark, the light from the television would catch the Vaseline and reflect off of it with the intensity of a mirror in the desert at high noon. The white Saturn-like rings that enveloped her lips gave the appearance of Al Jolson reincarnated—Al Jolson with an itchy ass.

And because she had just woken up, she would be completely disoriented and groggy, on a Rip Van Winkle sort of level. "Who … Oh, it's … Where did … You're up?

"No, Mom. I'm in bed asleep," I'd joke to mask the embarrassment for my friends.

Another level of shame was added the first time I had a girl over alone. I was a junior, and her name was Svetlana. She was a fresh-off-the-boat exchange student from Russia, with long, black hair, and oversized breasts for a high school student. I leapt at her quickly, knowing that in a few days she would discern who was on the "cool" list, and that I wasn't one of them. I took Svetlana to the stock car races to give the appearance I was more of a man's man because I figured she was used to tough Russian guys who had beards and swung axes. Afterward, she agreed to come back to my place, either because she liked me, or because of the language barrier. She thought I asked, "Should I take you home?"

Scraaatch! Scraaatch!

As soon as I heard the warning sound, I desperately tried to communicate to Svetlana that she should head to the bathroom in the basement. This was a daring move, as our bathroom had no internal walls. It was merely a freestanding toilet between the deep freeze and hot water heater. But I figured since she was Russian, a pail might be considered luxury.

Scraaatch! Scraaatch! "Who … Scott? … Oh, it's … What's going on?"

"Well, Mom, I'm entertaining a young lady."

"Where is she?"

"She was frightened off by the wolves."

"We have wolves?"

Just at that moment, Svetlana, having failed to find the downstairs "bathroom," came from the kitchen with an empty plate.

"Oh, is this her? Boy she's a looker. Hi, dear, how are you? Would you like a snack or some such? Don't hold your breath waiting for Scott to help. I've got some pot roast I can warm up for you toot-sweet if you're hungry. Are you hungry or are you just stretching your legs?"

It's hard enough for a native speaker to discern her long ramblings, much less a Russian.

Svetlana smiled and said in broken English, "Vut es dis 'pot roast'?"

Mom looked at me with concern. "Oh gosh, did you hear that? She talks goofy."

"*She* talks goofy," I thought to myself.

"She's a Russian exchange student, Mom."

"Oh, you don't say. From where?"

"Russia."

"Oh, oh," Mom declared, "the ones with the wall?"

"No, that's Germany."

"The ones who do so good at the Olympics gymnastics?"

"Yes, those Russians. Goodnight."

"Do you do gymnastic stuff, honey?"

"No, she doesn't."

"Well, you be careful down here. Holler if you need me."

And then, as the wandering minstrel show was making its way back to bed and I was about to curl up with Svetlana, somewhere in the darkness we heard … *Phhtt!*

"Boomer!"

I smiled as Svetlana turned to me and asked, "Vut es dis 'boomer'?"

Despite the news of Mom's wandering minstrel show, I managed to find someone to go to the prom with me. Her name is Trish, a blonde, extremely myopic Norwegian who was a member of the audio-visual club. The AV club ranked just above the chess club in popularity but well below the drama fags, which is why I suspect she agreed to accompany me to the event. We had gone out a few times for burgers and spent an evening navigating my mother's berserk minstrel show. Physically, I had never engaged in the act of intercourse with a girl, but Trish allowed me to get close one night in the car. This laid the perfect foundation for consummating our relationship on prom night.

I was excited, as it was going to be my first sexual experience with someone whose entire body wasn't covered in orange fur. Winnie and I were young, reckless lovers and therefore didn't practice safe sex; so I had no understanding of condom protocol, and made the mistake of going to the pharmacist at Walgreens for clarification. I thought, *Who better to educate me on the type and application of a condom than my friendly neighborhood pharmacist?* Sure, it'd be a little embarrassing, but far less than fumbling blindly in the dark the night of prom.

I don't know why it happened, but apparently back then pharmacists were in high demand in the Midwest. So companies gave financial incentives to pharmacists from the big cities to come work in the smaller towns. That particular year we were "blessed" with a volatile Chinese woman from New York City.

She seemed disoriented behind the counter. The computer was troubling for her; she yelled at it as if it were human and could speak Chinese. English was her second language, or third, so when she had something to say to an inanimate object, it was in her familiar tongue, and when speaking to customers, she used Chinese about half the time. There was a six-foot high glass partition that stood between the counter and the customers, which gave her the impression she had to yell to be heard. On top of this, every time a customer failed to understand her, she concluded it was an issue of volume, and would yell into the microphone that amplified through the store's PA system. So while you were innocently shopping for greeting cards or batteries it wasn't strange to hear:

"I say, putting on butt hoe! Rubbing on butt hoe, kay? 明白了吗 Two time a day! You not hearing me?"

Then you'd see someone scurry out of the store with their head down like a celebrity dodging paparazzi. As soon as a day later my mom would inform me that Vern Thompson had a rash on his nether region and wondered if I had heard anything more about it.

Walgreens had become a pharmaceutical circus: arthritis meds going this way, psychotic meds going that way. When you drive through at McDonald's you never know what's going to end up in your bag, and that's fine, because it all tastes the same anyway, but you really don't want your pharmacy to be a crapshoot.

Sadly, the day I went in was her first week on the job, and therefore I was unaware of this erratic behavior. In fact, I had remembered a friendly man working behind the counter the last time I was in there, and was looking forward to his nurturing bedside manner. So the immediate concern became her being a woman. *No problem*, I thought. *She's a professional and has probably dealt with far more delicate matters than this.*

I was standing in line with Neil Jorgensen—construction worker, beefy guy, dumb as a stump. We were in front of Cindy—gorgeous girl, cheerleader, dumb as a stump. Neil had been trying to strike up a conversation with Cindy when he was called to the counter. From what I could gather, something had gone wrong with his prescription card.

"不可以 给你 Prozac. No givy Prozac!"

Neil sort of looked back at us over his shoulder and then whispered, "Why?"

"这个卡错 Insurance bad! No good."

"Okay, thanks, no problem. I'll come back."

"You still buy?"

"No, too expensive."

"How about you suppositories? They cheap. Five dollar. You wa suppositories?"

"No thanks, I'll come back."

"You got cut in you ass. How gonna heal cut in ass? Bery tenda."

"Okay, thanks."

And because he started backing away, she raised her voice as she said, "Nothing be ashamed of. Many, many gay men have cut in ass."

Having relocated from New York, the pharmacist had a very comfortable relationship with homosexuality, the complete opposite relationship the fine people of Fargo had with it. And with that, Neil took off running for the exit.

And with great concern, the pharmacist yelled into the mic, "Mr. Jorgensen, no butt sex dis week. Asshole bery tenda."

"Hey." Cindy the cheerleader nodded her head and said, "You're next."

"Nex!" the crazy Chinese yelled into the microphone.

I crept to the window like Scooby-Doo making his way through a cemetery at midnight.

"Ummm … I need a condom," I whispered.

"No! Condom come in pack," her voice echoed through the aisles as the microphone had accidently been left on. "How many condom you need?"

My skin crawled as I felt every eye in the store turn to me. "Not many."

"What size? Sma, medium, lodge, exa lodge?"

I heard the word *tiny* come from Cindy and her giggling friend. A bout of my mother's hot flashes started to take over my body. I took a deep breath and guessed, "Medium."

"Guess again," I heard from the pack of giggling hyenas behind me.

While the Chinese woman was searching the rack behind her, I calmed my nerves by reminding myself that I was going to be having sex this weekend—and just because Cindy had sex *every* weekend shouldn't lessen my glory.

I needed to stay cool and ask this woman to turn off her microphone, and then simply ask her how one puts on a condom, not once considering that the directions might be on the package.

"Three packet. Four dollar, seventy-five cent."

As I pulled the money out of my wallet, I gingerly asked, "Excuse me, what's the best way to put these on?"

"Go on penis. Row down. Bery easy. Pull on penis."

Regrettably, I had forgotten to ask her to turn the mic off. I quickly looked around to confirm that everyone in line was doing their best to hold back laughter.

"Thank you," I said, and ran out the store in the same fashion as Neil Jorgensen. *Roll down. Pull on penis*, I recited to myself. *Roll down. Pull on penis.*

After a successful prom, Trish and I snuck into my bedroom and fumbled in the dark to rid ourselves respectively of peach chiffon and black polyester. Through a series of codified, fragmented sentences, we had agreed earlier in the evening that "it" was going to happen.

"Did you get any …" "You mean …" "Yeah." "Oh, yeah. Earlier." "Cool." "Cool."

Immediately after opening the condom wrapper I reminded myself of the Chinese woman's instructions: *Roll down. Pull on penis.* It unrolled out in my hand like a pat of warm butter. So far, so good, I thought. The *pull on penis* is where I ran into some trouble. No matter how hard you pull, tug, or cry, an unrolled condom is not going on anything.

In a panic, I slipped the condom into Trish's hand. "Here, put it on."

"You're supposed to put it on," she said.

"No, I think you are."

"No, I'm not," she declared. "Where'd you learn how to have scx, anyway?"

I imagined she didn't want to hear that I'd learned everything I knew about sex by fucking a stuffed bear. "The pharmacist taught me," I mumbled.

"What?"

I finally had to turn on my nightlight to see just what the hell was going on. Sometime in the moment of wrestling with my limp penis and the wiggly, wet condom is when Mom's wandering minstrel show wandered into my room. In retrospect, I'm shocked I hadn't heard the scratching.

"Scott? What … Who … What is …? Goodnight."

And with that she shuffled out. No scene. No discussion. No boomer. I think she was just proud that I had finally moved on from Winnie.

Trish and I never consummated our prom date. Actually, she ended up walking out. I disappointed Trish and became the laughing stock of the audio-visual club, an organization that was already the laughing stock of the entire school.

I decided to set aside my sexual quest and go back to the hobby I was actually good at: bowling. I started spending a lot of time down at the alley. Erv, the owner, was a natural born entertainer, and also owned a bar called JB's, which he used as his playground to perform. And it was here, on an intellectual level, that I began connecting the emotional weight of "love" and the physical act of "sex."

The bar was seven miles out, in Casselton, a farming town so small it didn't bother to have its population listed on its "Welcome to Casselton" sign. JB's is a traditional, dusty dive, with a small dance floor where local farmers with snap shirts and tan lines bring their wives to two-step. Once we turned nineteen, Tyler and I would occasionally go out there on weekends just to catch Erv's act, which included wacky song parodies and wildly comedic weather reports, news updates, and sports briefs. He was a comedic genius, and his wit rivaled anything I had ever heard on the television.

On the wall behind him were clocks displaying each time zone. After returning from an exhausting Greyhound bus trip to New York City, he added two hours to the Eastern time zone, claiming, "It's further away than you think."

One night he held a funeral for his pet rooster that had passed away. He placed a public invitation on the *Farmers Market* radio show and nearly everyone in town came to pay their respects. The bar was packed to overflowing, so people opened the doors and listened to the ceremony from the parking lot. He had the local taxidermist preserve the rooster, and then fitted it with a custom made tuxedo. The rooster sits on the back of the bar to this day.

It was here, one drunken night, that Allan Grossman revealed his secret to me. He said he wanted to release a heavy burden from his shoulders, but I had to promise not to pass judgment on him or tell anyone else, including his wife. My initial thought was, it's kind of late and I'd rather go home than have anything dumped on me that'll be fighting to get out the next time I'm drunk. But I agreed to hear him out.

He stared glossy-eyed for a moment and then launched into it. "For the last two years I've been getting paid to drive to Minneapolis once a month."

I waited patiently for the end of the sentence, the exciting, "danger" part that could never be revealed to anyone or he might die, but he just sat there. "That's it? That's your big secret?"

He looked down deep into the bottom of his beer and shook his head. "No." He paused again, not for affect, but from a true struggle to confront the truth. To say it out loud would make it all the more real. "I ... I ... I ... go there to let a rich woman spank me. No sex. She just strips me naked, bosses me around a little bit, and then makes me watch as she uses a vibrator on herself. That's it."

"The fuck?" I scanned the bar quickly with my eyes. "Allan, that's the type of thing you write on a napkin and slide across the table and then we burn it."

"No one heard me."

"Well, sadly, I did."

"God, I feel so much better," he sighed.

"You're married, Allan."

"There's no sex."

"Still, you think Sarah would be okay with that?"

"Scott, it paid for my college. And gives me the freedom to do my writing."

This woman has apparently financed Allan's dream of becoming a writer. Unfortunately, it hasn't afforded him the *talent* of a writer. Allan received his BFA in creative writing from an agricultural college. If you want to master the science of sheep shit you go there; if you want to learn how to craft a brilliant sentence, you go anywhere else. I must hand it to him, however; Allan writes despite his lack of talent. He writes and has me read his material, which is consistently poor, not to mention he writes about very safe, sterile stuff like wheat and snowmobiles. Why he doesn't write about women spanking his naked ass, I have no idea. He tried submitting some freelance stories to the local paper but never heard back. He wasn't rejected so much as he was basically ignored by the editor—because the Midwestern approach to delivering bad news is to avoid the person for the rest of your life.

Once I got over the initial shock and awe of Allan's secret, he told me there was more. Something he wanted to ask me, a request.

"I don't want to hear it. Please don't tell me. In fact, if I could go back in time and take back hearing about your hairy, naked ass being spanked, I would."

"It's a favor."

"I think you're out of favors."

"Scott, seriously."

"Seriously, I just did you the favor of not puking on you.

"I need you to take over for me next month."

"Take over what?"

"I can't do it next month, and when I told her, she got very upset and said she was going to find someone else to replace me. Permanently. Scott, I need that income. I can't get a day job; it would ruin my writing career."

"What writing career?"

Apparently before the marriage, he told his wife, Sarah, that he had received an inheritance from his grandfather, which would afford him the time to write and still be able to help with household expenses. Sarah is an elementary school teacher and had a conference that she wanted Allan to attend with her, but it happened to fall on the same day he was scheduled to meet the Minneapolis woman.

"Ask her to change the date," I suggested.

"She wouldn't, so I asked her if a buddy of mine could take over."

"Hell, no."

"I can't lose this gig, Scott."

"Listen, I'm not, uhm … as much as you think I might be, I'm not all that versed in the ways of sex."

"All the better. She likes the young, naïve type."

"Nope."

"It's a quick trip to Minneapolis."

"No, I don't think so, man. I'm sorry."

"There's a thousand bucks in it for you."

As soon as I arrived in Minneapolis, I called the woman; Ginger was her name. Allan instructed me to go straight to the motel—yes, *motel*—but I had yet to talk with her and was nervous about getting naked in front of someone I hadn't made contact with.

She picked up the phone and said, "Yes?"

In all my twenty-one years of calling people, not once had anyone answered by saying "Yes?" I realize it may be a common practice for the big city types, but this was my first. In Fargo we rarely stray from "Hello." In fact, we never stray from it. "Hello" is what we say. If you factor in our accent, you might actually hear the word *Yelloooo*, but in our heads it's *Hello*.

Obviously, "Yes?" is the kind of recklessness in a phone greeting that will eventually corrupt a person and lead him down a path of aberrant sexuality. Or I guess the reverse could happen: aberrant sexuality could lead to impersonal phone greetings. I figured it was only a matter of time after my experience with Ginger that I would be answering the phone with a "What's up?" or "Howdy." And friends would grow suspicious and wonder if I was involved in drugs or something.

I nervously cleared my throat and responded, "Ahhh … yelloo, this is Scott." Silence from her end. "Allan's friend?" Nothing. "The one who is replacing him this month … he said he had talked to you?"

Finally she said in a gruff, Smokey voice that sounded irritated with this whole thing and was planning to take it out on me, "Room 24."

"Great. Okay, I'll be there in a jiff. Should I—" And with that she hung up.

The Cottontail Motel sat a mile off the highway, but there was nothing white or cottony about it, and in no way did it convey anything rabbit-like, unless there's a species of rabbit that eats human flesh. There were only three cars in the lot: a piece of shit Toyota, a minivan, and a white Lexus, which I assumed was Ginger's. I backed into a spot just in case I needed to make a quick getaway. Not that my Dodge Dart could get anywhere quickly, but I felt better about the prospect of skipping the reverse process if the shit should go down. And I was convinced shit would be going down, which is why I brought my mom's pepper spray.

I knocked on the door and waited. And waited more. A family with three screaming kids was piling into the minivan. The father looked up at me suspiciously after I had been standing at the door for a few minutes. It seemed as though he knew what was behind door 24 and felt sorry for me; or he was an undercover cop posing as a father of three screaming kids and was about to take me down.

I turned back to the door and knocked again. From within I thought I heard a verbal response that expressed either "Come in" or "Hold on a minute." I interpreted it as "Hold on," but the pressure of the cop's eyes forced me to turn the handle and push the door open a single inch.

"Yelloooo?" I whispered into the room, which appeared to be lit only by the sunlight that snuck through the crack in the door.

"Come," she said. Not "Come in," just "Come," another sign that I was dealing with big city lingo.

I opened the door just enough to slip in, and then shut it immediately to conceal any evidence of nefarious activity from the cop, who was now staring at me from behind the wheel of the minivan, which was already loaded with kids, but for some reason was not backing out. The room was tiny and smelled like dust. An oversized lamp sat on the nightstand, capturing the clouds of smoke from her cigarette. If age makes you a professional, she was a seasoned professional. Allan had failed to convey just how unattractive she was. I had envisioned Mrs. Robinson—shy, reclined on the bed in a silky green slip, with painted nails and a long, blondish wig—not *Mr.* Robinson.

Backing out of the deal with the simple phrase "Did you order a large pepperoni?" was on the tip of my tongue until I thought of Allan's desperate pleading about not "ruining his writing career." Considering the state of his "career," there was little incentive for me to stay. But I did.

"Have you done this before?" she asked. It was her first complete sentence.

What did she mean by *this*? I wondered. Had I met an older woman in a motel before? Had I ever had sex before? "Yes," I said, not sure which question I was answering.

"Hmmm," she pondered. "Doesn't seem like it."

"Well, I have," I said defensively.

"You look like a shivering little boy."

"I'm no longer a boy. I'm in college."

"You're not a fraternity kind of boy, so what? You must still be living with Mommy and Daddy?"

"Just to save money. Next year I—"

"What's your major?"

"General studies right now."

"What do you want to be when you grow up?"

"I want to … well, I kind of wouldn't mind being an actor."

"Kind of? You want to be in actor in Fargo? How does that work? Don't you need to go to the big city or somewhere?"

"Well—"

"Why you majoring in general studies if you want to be an actor?"

"It didn't seem practical to major in theater."

"So wasting your parents' money on general studies seems practical?"

I simply shrugged and looked away, hoping the badgering would stop.

"Are you afraid, college boy?"

"No," I said, which was not entirely true, as my eyes had caught an extra-large suitcase filled with black foreign objects that were adorned with silver studs.

The line of questioning was over. She dropped her cigarette into a can of Diet Fresca, and in a commanding voice said, "Take off you pants."

And I did, followed by my shirt and underwear.

"What are you doing?"

"Taking off my clothes," I stuttered.

"Did I ask you to take off your shirt and underwear?"

I had just turned an awkward moment into a monumentally awkward moment. I could have sworn Allan said he was naked. Didn't he say he was naked? Oh God, I'm unnecessarily naked!

As I was about to pull my underwear back on, she stopped me and went to the suitcase. She pulled out a pair of black, high-top Converse sneakers and said, "Put these on."

For a moment I was relieved, thinking we might engage in an innocent game of naked one-on-one or H-O-R-S-E, but the next thing she pulled out of the case wasn't a basketball.

"Get on the bed," she snapped.

I bent over and laced up my shoes for the big game and then sheepishly crawled onto the bed.

With a magician-like flourish she had pulled a riding crop from the suitcase. "No, stand up," she said, punctuating it with a smack to the mattress.

I scurried to my feet, not wanting to be punished. In her other hand was the end of a rope, the length yet to be determined because it was still snaking its way out of the suitcase. She gave my penis a friendly little tap with the riding crop.

"Does it get hard?"

I croaked, "Yes." Which was more or less true.

She looked at me in disbelief and snorted as if Allan's penis was continually at full attention. She knelt on the mattress and moved closer and closer. I pulled my hips back. "Ummm, I was told that you were just going to, you know, spank me."

Her tired gray eyes looked up at me until I moved my hips b.
in place. I didn't want to move my hips back, but I'm midwesterne
everyone else's needs are more important than mine. Allan needed
to maintain an undiscovered writing career, and this strange woman
needed to put my penis in her mouth.

"Oh look, you're a man after all," she said and then proceeded
to wrap the rope around my balls, individually, and up the shaft,
leaving me with a purple, throbbing head.

The mind is a powerful thing, even mine, but in that moment
I pushed its thought capacity to its limit. Worlds of scenarios were
playing and overlapping one another in my head. I was unaware that
this type of sexual activity existed, and wondered if it could even be
considered sex. This certainly could not be "making love." I was even
saddened a bit when I considered that Ginger was probably using
this "sex" to patchwork a hole in her life. But what remained in the
forefront was the puzzling thought: Allan has had his penis bound
like a rodeo calf, and all he can think to write about is the beauty
of a trickling creek?

Ginger was into control. She not only got turned on by controlling
my penis, but also wanted to manipulate my emotions. "What would
your parents think if they saw you like this?" she asked.

"They're divorced," I admitted, quicker than I had ever done
before in my life. Finally my parents' divorce may actually be of
some benefit, I thought.

She picked up the phone with a smirk and asked, "What would
your mom think if you told her what's happening right now?"

I wanted to warn Ginger that that tactic would backfire on her
with someone like my mom, but realized she would never believe
me, so I played up the emotions for her. "No, don't call her please!"
I cried.

"What's your number?"

I pretended to give it to her unwillingly, she dialed, and after
someone picked up, she handed the phone to me. "It's a woman."

"Mom?" I asked into the receiver. "Yeah, well … Uh huh …
No … Yes … No…"

Ginger interrupted Mom's rant, "Tell her what's happening."

"Mom ... Mom ... Mom, I need to ... I put them in the hamper like you told me, but Mom, I'm suppose to tell you that I'm tied up in a motel room right now by a ... I don't know ... I don't ... I realize that but I don't know ..."

"What did she say," a desperate Ginger asked.

I held the phone to my chest while Mom continued talking. "She said she has Tater Tots in the FryDaddy and wants to know when I'll be home." This was not the response Ginger was hoping for. Her face dropped.

Not satisfied with my job, Ginger held her hand out for the phone.

"Mom, I'm handing the phone over to ... my friend."

She grabbed the phone. "This is Ginger and I ... No... Well, sort of ..."

This was the first time since entering the motel that I became comfortable. And comfortable was the exact opposite feeling the phone call was supposed to invoke. I laughed to myself wondering what path Mom was leading the conversation down. Western bacon cheeseburgers? Vern Thompson's ass rash?

Ginger was finally offered a moment to respond: "I'm lactose intolerant ... Oh really, let me get my purse."

I was proud witnessing Mom take down a big-city, socialite-Sadist with her patented, rapid-fire banality. Finally—a purpose for her talent.

Ginger was scribbling something down on the back of an envelope that was housing some kind of bill. I never imagined my mother saying anything worthy of taking note. But as Ginger scribbled she also mumbled, which led me to realize she was jotting down a recipe for cheese-free potato chip casserole.

I pointed at my throbbing penis and she nodded for me to untie it.

Twenty minutes later I was dressed, headed home, and looking forward to leftover Tater Tots casserole. Ginger let me off easy. Nothing further happened, and I suppose I have my mom to thank for that. It's a 243-mile drive from Minneapolis to Fargo, allowing plenty of time to burn through the radio stations, only to conclude there is nothing but country. The first song I heard immediately made me think of JB's bar. Sure, I always went there for Erv's hijinks, but secretly, I stayed to watch the dancing.

You haven't seen grace and poetry in motion until you've witnessed an older farm couple two-step. It's an experience that words cannot communicate, but seeing it firsthand could turn an atheist to God. I don't think there is any greater expression of love for a farmer's wife than to be asked by her husband for a dance. But they don't ask, necessarily. I've studied it a million times. He simply slides his chair out from the table in a way that's measured and proper; it's slightly different from getting up to grab another beer or use the restroom. He doesn't offer a hand, as such, but simply nods and moves to the floor, and when their bodies come together, there's no awkward moment of waiting for the downbeat like careless strangers might. They don't talk, but occasionally will exchange a look coupled with a tender smile. Shuffle, shuffle, gliiiide. Shuffle, shuffle, gliiiide. Their bodies appear to float on a cushion of air, yet are in constant communication with the ground. After all, the ground, the land, and the soil are something they understand; they've spent a lifetime up to their elbows in it.

On that dark stretch of highway back to Fargo, having just experienced a crude form of seduction, I figured there's got to be something more to sex than just the sex. Somewhere between the childhood exploration of playing doctor, the fumbling teenagers in the dark, and the craziness of Ginger, there had to be more, but I was unable to find it. I tried, but had very few takers. And the ones that did "take" were exciting for a moment, but then anytime after that moment we were just trying to recreate more of the same. Was it because we weren't in love? What was it? I suspected the farm couple on JB's dance floor knew what it was all about. They twirl and sway as her hand rests gently in his, both hands worn to the bone with hard work, but soft to one another's touch. Shuffle, shuffle, gliiiide. Shuffle, shuffle, gliiiide.

Jane Peterson, Svetlana, Trish, Ginger, and even Winnie were all wonderful sexual encounters in their own way, but my dream is to someday experience a little of the shuffle, shuffle, gliiiide.

NINTH STREET
Kuntz

As my car crosses over Ninth Street, it hits me that the southwest corner has been vacant for most of the time I've lived in Fargo. The last business I remember being there was the car lot. It was my junior year when a South Dakota man bought the old medical center parking lot to sell cars. There it was one day out of the blue: KUNTZ. A huge neon sign advertising the new used car lot. And it *wasn't* pronounced with a long *u*. I'm not kidding. His name was Henry Kuntz, an overweight bald man who favored wearing white suits and smoking cigars. It's believed we are all created from the image of God, but when you look at Henry Kuntz you really hope that's not true. As it turned out, it was a Polish family named Kuntzski whose great grandfather didn't want to have a name that stigmatized the family, so he dropped "ski" off the end making it simply "Kuntz." There you go. No more stigma.

The owner had a local commercial that ran continuously during the evening news, and like all good local advertising, he would shout his name over and over again, "Kuntz!" "Come on down to Kuntz!" "I'm Frank Kuntz."

It's surprising with such an unfortunate name as Kuntz that he'd have such a large sign. And it flashed "KUNTZ … KUNTZ … KUNTZ." It was beautiful. There was a collective community gasp: the adults hated it, the organized religions revolted, even the

Lutherans, but the kids loved it. "Kuntz." It rolled off our juvenile tongues like Mountain Dew. It was a free pass to talk dirty in front of our parents: "Kuntz!"

The sign became the target of ridicule every time Tyler and I drove past. We challenged each other to come up with the best tag line for their competitor's television ads: "I got screwed with one of those Kuntz cars," "There's some fishy business going down at Kuntz." And my personal favorite: "The Chrysler dealership down the street has prices that lick Kuntz."

"Scott Allen!" my mom would snap while incorporating my middle name, which she used whenever she meant business.

"What? I was just talking about the car place, Kuntz. You know, Kuntz. Kuntz on the corner of Ninth? That's the Kuntz I was referring to," I defended myself, trying to get as many in as possible.

Kuntz closed after six months, having sold not one single lemon. We like to think our jokes drove him out of town, but I really doubt it. It's more likely that they had to leave because Fargo doesn't like change; and they don't like foreigners, especially when they're "Kuntz" from South Dakota.

So now the parking lot is vacant, except in the summers, when the high school pom-pom girls hold a car wash to raise money for … I don't know what exactly—pom-poms perhaps? Judging from the halftime shows, they should invest in a choreographer. Currently, one of the ladies from the church auxiliary is working out the dance numbers for them. Either that, or Reverend Sonnenberg himself.

Now, during harvest season, farmers from the surrounding counties gather together in the vacant lot and sell fresh vegetables from their gardens. But as a child I was lucky enough to pick my own vegetables right out of the ground, because my summers were spent staying on my maternal grandparents' farm. The farm sat just outside the small town of Ellendale where my father's parents also happened to live.

Starting at the age of six Dad and Mom would drive me to the farm, where I would stay for the entire summer vacation. Usually I would sleep during the car trips to their house—when I wasn't busy peeing into a bottle. I have a very small bladder, and into my teens was still wetting the bed. The trip to the farm was only two hours, but my need to pee happened every twenty minutes.

"Pull your swanse out and stick it in the bottle, Scottie," my dad suggest as an alternative to stopping.

I don't know why he called my penis a "swanse," or where he picked the term up, but he was unique that way. He always had a funny phrase and looked for any opportunity to tease people. Despite his struggles with alcoholism, he was a charming and witty guy who people loved. As soon as I was balancing on the backseat and had my swanse in the bottle, he would swerve quickly, throwing me off balance.

"Whoa, just missed that skunk that darted out." And then he would roar with laughter while watching through the rearview mirror as my naked butt and swanse struggled to gain control.

"Richard!" my mom would protest. "You're going to make him pee all over the seat."

"Pinch it, son. Pinch the ol' swanseroony! Don't let it loose on the seat."

"Dad! Stop it," I would say, trying not to laugh, which I knew would only encourage him.

"Whoops! Squirrel that time," he would say as my body flung against the adjacent door.

The farm sat two miles off the highway and connected with a gravel road. As soon as I heard the click of the gravel under the car, my heart would jump. Not only was I excited about arriving, but also, once we hit gravel my dad usually let me steer the car while sitting between his legs. My feet didn't reach the pedals, but that didn't matter; the power of the wheel was exhilarating enough.

"Right down the middle, Son," my dad would whisper in my ear as he gave it a little gas. "Bring it home."

It was fascinating the stuff you could learn on a farm. Things like … death. Once a week my grandma and I would butcher about six chickens. Regardless of my age, it was a horrifying event to experience. First, you have to catch the chicken, which can be tricky because … well, they're chickens, and they flap about a bit like chickens are wont to do. But Grandma had this long metal hook that she used to catch one of their legs. They try to dodge this as much as they can, but chickens have sort of limited dodging skills, outside of flapping. Next, she would hold the bird like a football under her arm while she grabbed it by the neck with the other hand, and without a flinch of remorse, would ring its neck in one little flick of her wrist, a kind of circular motion, like coiling a garden hose.

Next, she took it over to the workbench, and with a butcher knife, lopped off its head … *foooom*! But as soon as she threw it to the ground, it would spring to life as if it had been sleeping, and chopping its head off somehow woke it up. Very strange. Some weird irony, which my young mind couldn't comprehend. Killing it seemed to bring it back to life. Now I may have it wrong—it was a long time ago and I was young—but that's the type of image that sticks with you pretty accurately, just like walking into the sheep barn and catching your uncle masturbating.

While I was standing dumbfounded, the decapitated chicken would head directly at me. "Ahhhhhhhhhhhh!" It would flop around me in a circular pattern, splattering blood everywhere, as I stood horrified, trying not to wet myself. And if it ever got too close to me, I would scream like a little girl. But it was sort of a choked scream as if I were afraid to attract the attention of the dead chicken—as if its bloody corpse might stagger toward the sound.

"Help me. Grandma, help me. Help me." My lips never moved. I sounded like a ventriloquist. I don't know why I thought the chicken could hear me; its ears were in a bucket.

She'd always say, "Oh, don't worry; it's dead."

"Then why is it still flying?"

"Nerves."

"Kill it again," I would plead while clinching my tiny penis to block the flow.

"It's just a little blood."

Then she'd throw down another one. Chicken after chicken. At any given time there could be four chickens circling me in varying degrees of nerve damage. It was not unlike Indians doing a war dance around you while you're tied to a stake, I imagine.

Once all the life was drained from one of their bodies, Grandma would pick it up by its legs, dip it into a bucket of boiling water, and pluck it bald. Wet, dead chicken feathers always proved to have an interesting smell, especially when mixed with the scent of my fresh urine. Then she would slice it open, pull its guts out, pop it in the oven, and an hour later we'd be eating it.

My grandmother was in charge of chickens, geese, the garden, canning every fruit and vegetable known to man, and cooking—including her own birthday cakes. And during the harvest, cooking involved lunch for twelve men and a regular flow of coffee with cookies. My job was to drive the thermos and plate of goodies out to the field. I was ten when I first had to drive the old pickup truck with the dashboard I couldn't see over unless I stood up. It was a four-speed with a large, black, greasy stick shift that stuck out of the floorboard. It took both hands and the weight of my entire body to shift from first gear to second, so it's not hard to believe that third and fourth never saw the light of day while I was behind the wheel. Since shifting required that I take both hands off the steering wheel, I usually just crept in first gear through the cow pasture to the men in the field, going at a rate of speed too slow for the speedometer to register.

After my parents divorced and my dad moved out of Fargo, my grandfather was the only father figure I had—and he was a good one. He had a powerful and commanding presence, and when he stood, he covered every acre of his land. The farm was handed down to him by his father. He worked on it from the time he was old enough to carry a pail until he retired at the age of sixty-three. He was born in the room that became the only bedroom he would ever occupy.

He taught me how to belch and to suck a steak bone dry. He also taught me to chew tobacco. Worn away by a can of Copenhagen, the front left pocket of my grandpa's denim shirt had a white circle pattern. The spot was always there, which kept me wondering if maybe he had only one shirt. For awhile, I concluded that they were made that way so you knew where to keep your can.

His process of taking a pinch of chew was an art form, and I would stare as if the "Mona Lisa" were being created before my eyes. Following two taps on top of the can with his right thumb and a twist of the cover, a wave of mint would fill the air. His big, thick, sun-dried fingers managed their way through the tobacco, searching for the perfect pinch. And every pinch was perfect. A shake. And once positioned between the cheek and gum, he'd wipe his fingers clean on his thigh, a swipe with the thumb in front and the pointer finger up along the seam. I was only nine or ten years old, too young for tobacco, but a final step in his routine was always to offer me a pinch. I suspect he wanted me to feel like a man. And I did. I felt like him.

"Not today," I would say, as if tomorrow I might consider taking up the habit.

He told me the spit fertilized his soil and the tobacco fertilized his soul. For a few years I thought this Copenhagen guy might be Jesus, but Pastor Sonnenberg's shirts never had any white circles on them, and I rarely saw him spit, so I figured against it. One day, I decided to take Grandpa up on his offer. I took a pinch and stuck it between my cheek and gums, just like he did. I wiped my finger and thumb off, just like he did. And I spit, just like he did. Then I threw up—for about forty-five minutes—which he never did.

The farm didn't have many, if any, modern advantages. It was not unlike the farm on the television show *Green Acres*, except we didn't have to climb a pole to talk on the phone. But we did share a phone line with the neighbors. So when you picked up the receiver and didn't hear a dial tone, you'd often hear the Andersons complaining about something to their son who lived in Montana. It was a way to become very intimate with your neighbors. We also had an outhouse for many years because water was scarce that far out of town. Once the indoor plumbing was installed, we had to conserve water by not flushing the toilet unless a severe "movement" had arrived. And not until later was there a TV to watch, but it didn't matter because I could shoot cows with my BB gun.

Both my grandpa and grandma expressed emotion and love in simple ways, ways that you had to keep a close lookout for; otherwise you might've missed them. Grandma cooked the meals and did the dishes afterward, but once in awhile, as she was drying, Grandpa might grab one or two dishes and put them in the cupboard as a way of saying, "Thank you for marrying me and sticking by my side for fifty years." And in the same way, after twelve straight hours of harvesting, Grandpa might come home to find the pigs had already been fed, which was my grandma's way of saying, "Thank you for asking me to marry you, and I love you too." They were strong, hearty people who were frightened by nothing. They were nothing like my parents.

My grandmother was particularly tough for a woman. She would grab a bug and squish it between her fingers without the aid of a Kleenex or a scream. If a snake found its way into the pantry, she would grab it by the neck and throw it out the window before I had time to run to a corner of the house and whimper. Her strength is what made it all the more difficult to accept, when ten short years later she could no longer recognize my face. For me, my grandmother died the day Alzheimer's took control. We became strangers. All that was left were memories and photographs.

I'm not sure what was more difficult to deal with: my grandmother's sudden inability to make coffee or my grandfather's denial of it. Whenever she looked across the dinner table and asked, "Who is he?" my grandfather would immediately have a litany of questions for my mom about the ingredients of the three-bean casserole—a dish he had been eating all his life and could have made himself while blindfolded in the back of a moving vehicle. It is no surprise that my grandmother outlasted him on this earth. Her disease killed him before it killed her.

The summer after my grandfather's death was my last summer working on the farm. I was in my freshman year at college and landed my first "real" job in the workplace. I was employed at the Olive Garden, Fargo's answer to fine dining. It sat on the southwest corner of Ninth Street. My mom pulled some strings and got me in, thank God, otherwise I don't know how I would have cracked their hiring code. And why she saw this as a favor to me I will never know. She assumed that because she loved the restaurant business, her son would naturally feel the same way. I would rather have laid railroad ties across the state than cater to coupon carriers who suddenly become extravagant in their demands simply because they see tablecloths and assume they're in a four-star restaurant.

I put in a week's worth of training by "shadowing" another waiter, but never actually had my own table. My mom suggested I should have been trained longer, but no training in the world would have prepared me for the quantity of trailer park trash who filed through that dump, riding their high horses.

One particular family, let's call them the Jackasses, was the third table of my first shift working alone. You know the type: Dad, a wife-beater, wearing jean shorts and flip-flops revealing toenails that look like they've been used to cut lumber. The wife usually tips the scale around two hundred pounds but still wears a bikini top in public. The kids, of which there are usually three or four too many, have cherry Kool-Aid rings around their mouths and enough Cheetos residue on their hands to make it look like they're wearing orange gloves. These people are the ones you don't know personally but may recognize from driving past the trailer park or being subjected to their monopolizing an aisle at the Target in South Fargo. The "folks" are accustomed to eating at Hardees, or more likely, in their El Camino on the way home from Hardees, while the kids cling to the sides of the pickup bed. So to them, a trip to the Olive Garden is like a trip to the Plaza. They plop down like the king and queen of England, with their five glasses of water and forty breadsticks, and expect the royal treatment.

The first two tables on my first day working alone were a complete disaster because the patrons clearly hadn't read the word *trainee* on my badge and were completely insensitive to my unfamiliarity with the menu and the specials, and where the silverware was kept. So, by the time the Jackasses crawled onto their seats, I was a mere thirty minutes into my shift, yet nearly at the end of my patience. Not a good emotional position to be in with six hours still remaining.

By the time I got back to the Jackasses' table with five very heavy glasses of water, they had already devoured an entire basket of breadsticks, and I'm sure it was as big a shock to the other patrons as it was to me that the basket itself hadn't been eaten.

"What the hell's this shit?" asked King Jackass, fishing for the lemon wedge as if the hostess had fitted him with boxing gloves.

I tried rolling my eyes the entire five minutes I was standing there waiting for him to retrieve the lemon, but it's more of a single gesture, so I switched to loudly tapping my foot.

"What the hell's this?" he repeated as if everyone in the establishment hadn't heard him the first time.

I looked to Queen Jackass for some sort of confirmation that the her husband had, in fact, left his senses, but all I got was a *Well, don't just stand there* sort of look, as if he were holding a dead mouse.

"We in the trade like to call that a wedge of lemon." I used "we" to disperse any blame that was about to be placed on me for its lack of shape, size, or tartness.

"The hell's it doin' here?"

"We put that in there to make it seem special for you, so it doesn't taste like you're back home suckin' on the garden hose." That went too far, I realize.

"I've been around and I know you're supposed to put a lime in there, not lemon. You're just lazy. Git me a wedge of lime," he shouted, like I was a speaker box at the drive-thru.

"Oh, yeah? You want a lime? You want me to *git* you a wedge of lime?"

"Make it five wedges," he challenged.

"Oh, ya'll want a wedge of lime, do you?"

That sent me over the edge. Had I not put in a full thirty minutes already, maybe I could have dealt with them, but at this point my nerves were frayed. The third table of my first shift, nonetheless, and these animals all wanted a wedge of lime. The kids gazed at me with toothless smiles as if Dad had just asked for a pound of caramel corn.

"Yup."

It was too much. He had challenged my sense of work ethic by calling me lazy. I spent the better part of my youth shoveling pig manure, toting bucket-loads of grain into feeders, and entire afternoons shooting things with my BB gun. I was anything but lazy.

Just to fuck with them, I said, "That'll be a dollar per wedge."

You could see the blood leave their faces.

"Yeah, that's right. A buck a wedge! So that'll be five lime wedges, will it?"

In retrospect I feel bad, but an emotional battering is better than a homicide. He's lucky I hadn't brought my BB gun to work or I'd just be finishing up my jail sentence now.

Mitch, the manager who had been keeping an eye on me, recognized the extended delay after a standard "water drop" and made his way over to the table.

"Is there a problem here?"

"No," I quickly replied.

But Mr. Jackass overlapped me with "Damn tootin' there is. We want lime wedges 'stead of lemon."

"Everyone!" I added, trying to better illuminate their crime.

"Okay, Scott will bring those right over to you."

"Will that cost extra?" asked Lady Jackass.

"For …" Mitch asked with certain disbelief, like he might be the brunt of a practical joke.

"Limes. Are they more money?"

"Ahhh … no, on the house."

Master Jackass pointed a stern finger at me and said, "For a trainer, you sure don't know much."

Mitch and I shared a glance down at my "Trainee" badge and then to one another before excusing ourselves.

Once behind kitchen doors Mitch said, "Scott, the first thing you must learn is that the customer is always right."

"No they're not. He just called me a trainer, which is the opposite of right."

"Just get them what they want."

"They only want limes cause they think lemons are wrong. All they have to do is look around. Every table has lemons."

"The customer is always right," he repeated and walked off.

What definition of "right" was he using? And how far would he take this stupid retail axiom? I wondered if Mr. Jackass would still be in the "right" if he had Mitch's wife bent over the salad bar. Would it be "right" to lather her breasts with blue cheese dressing and have his dog lick them dry? What would it take for the customer to be wrong?

In my eyes, being poor was no excuse for their distasteful and unappreciative behavior. My family was poor, too. My mom shopped at the Salvation Army, and my brother and I appreciated any warm meal that was placed before us. If I were one of those kids, a lemon in my water would be the cherry on top of an evening that included a meal with both a mother and a father.

At the end of the dinner, Mr. Jackass decided "all you can eat" meant "all you can shove under your shirt." I caught him at the door just after collecting the fifty-cent tip he left me. I let him get away with the lime incident, but no way in hell was he walking out of there with breadsticks. Not on my watch.

"Excuse me, sir. Did you want a doggie bag for those breadsticks?"

"What breadsticks?"

"The ones in the basket."

"What basket?"

"The one under your shirt. Just behind the grease stain."

"No, I'll just take 'em like this."

"I'm sorry sir, but while the breadsticks are technically free, the basket is not."

"Oh, I didn't know that."

"Well, now you do."

And then he proceeded to stuff all twelve of them into the baby stroller.

"Is a dozen gonna be enough for you?" I said at the top of my voice. I hadn't noticed the entire restaurant was watching, so I continued. "How's twelve dozen sound? Tell you what, why don't you just back your El Camino up to the kitchen, and we'll load it up."

Mitch came running across the restaurant. "Scott! Scott! Customer's right!"

"Better yet, just park your trailer in our lot, and that way you'll have a lifetime supply of breadsticks and lime wedges!"

The next thing I remember was being face down under a table covered in primavera sauce, which happened to be the special. Who knew?

That was the last day I stepped foot in the Garden.

There were two things I learned from my grandparents. First, just because my mother and father got divorced didn't necessarily mean a lifelong marriage was impossible. Second, I learned to appreciate the measure of good work ethic. We worked our hands to the bone every day from sunrise through closing the cattle gate before going to bed. Their garden was half an acre large and supplied food that would last through the winters. But it didn't come without an exhausting amount of watering, weeding, tilling, planting, and picking. When you headed to the garden to work, you didn't bring a sack lunch; lunch was spread out before you in the soil. With one hand you could pull off an ear of corn, husk it, and eat it raw while you pulled weeds with the other. Labor on a farm is, for the most part, tranquil and meditative. There is no one around for miles. Its working code is built on autonomy. Cattle and pigs are the only customers a farmer has, and rarely do they complain about not having a lime in their water. I guess an excessive amount of isolation can promote a lack of patience for other people. Apparently it did for me. I was never able to go back to the customer-is-always-right type of job. Instead, I spent my summers working for Tyler's father, who owned a construction company. We got to work with our hands and build houses with a crew of maybe two or three others. It came easily for me. I didn't understand how to work with a restaurant full of customers, but *this* I understood. The farmer and the carpenter have much in common. Sweat. Toil. Vigor. These were the qualities instilled in me by a childhood of pastoral summer vacations.

I'll have no fonder memories in life than those summers spent on the farm. The images and odors are as strong now as the day they were realized. And the sound of tires on a gravel road will always make me believe we are headed to a wonderful place.

EIGHTH STREET
Caskets 'n' More

I pull over at Eighth Street to restack a box that has slid off the top of the pile in my passenger seat, dumping its contents over the dashboard and floor. The rain has made the vacant lot on the south side of the street a virtual mud bath. After the old supermarket was torn down, the lot remained empty for three years. Just recently they broke ground to put up something new. I don't know what exactly, and for some reason my mother hasn't informed me—usually, that type of information is of utmost importance.

As I shut the door after recovering the contents of the upturned box, I stand on the sidewalk looking into the muddy construction pit. The rain has downgraded to mist. On the corner and five yards in from the street is a sign displaying the name of the construction company, and in a print too fine to penetrate the precipitation is what looks to be the name of the new business. I walk tiptoe through the muddy puddles to get a better look at the announcement on the sign: "Coming Soon ... *Caskets 'n' More*." Hmmm. Strange. Only in Fargo would someone come up with a concoction like that.

Part of me wants to postpone my trip to find out what the *more* will be. What *more* do you need? If I'm buying a casket for my aunt Myrtle's dead body, there's really nothing *more* they can offer me, except maybe an act of God. I mean, can I walk in and say, "Yeah, I need a casket and a pound of bratwurst." How far are they going to go? Can a guy get his tires rotated, I wonder? Caskets 'n' More? Maybe they misspelled *gasket*.

As I grab the sign for support and sludge my way down to the sidewalk, a certain melancholy clinches my stomach. I fold my arms across my chest to fight off the chill and nearly feel as if I might, in fact, start to bawl. It's contained for a moment as I take in a deep breath of the cool, wet air. My hair is now dripping a bit. The neighborhood, the street, and the houses in front of me are so familiar to my daily routine that I never take note of them; but in this very moment they seem to pop off the landscape. The details rush at me so fast that I feel overwhelmed. I can't take them all in: the scent of jasmine from the Hendersons' bushes that line the weathered picket fence; the *8* on their house number dangles loose; a large crack runs up the cement of their driveway; a cellar door ramps off the north side of the house. A cellar door? How long have they had a cellar door? Forever? They still have their storm windows on. Or did they just put them on? I don't know. For some reason, the not knowing takes my breath from me. I quickly turn back to the construction pit in an attempt to stop the barrage of images. A deep breath, and now another one … and again. Behind the sign I notice Helen's house. I smile at the thought of her and feel a warmth tingle down my arms and into my fingers, which clutch at my jacket sleeves.

Helen lives in a small house behind the empty lot. On Mondays I had Cub Scouts. The quickest route to Uncle Dwight's trailer from my den meeting was to cut through Helen's yard. Quickest, that is, if Helen wasn't in need of having suntan oil rubbed on her back. Helen was the type of woman that you didn't want to ask, "How are you doing?" because she would tell you. But I didn't mind Helen, because it didn't matter to her that I was only eight; she talked to me like I was just another adult. I heard things I'm positive my parents would not have approved. I was getting an education on the seedy underbelly of life.

Helen was probably in her seventies, but with her withered, overtanned skin, looked more like she was in her nineties. She was never without a cigarette and a glass of scotch, both in the same

hand. And when she smoked, she *smoked*. She drew it in all the way
to her toes. Helen was skinny in a sickly way, yet had a little gut that
hung over her bikini bottom, which she wore every day during the
summer, with a gaudy blonde wig. At the time, I was too young to
make an assessment, but later it was clear to me that a deep-seated
depression had worn away at her sanity. Some days were better than
others, but every day was littered with moments of schizophrenic
banter.

"How am I doing?" she asked in her deep baritone voice. "I'll
tell ya how I'm doing. This piece of shit I call a husband, this rotting
lump of cancer I sleep next to every night, brags about his six-figure
Citibank job. Well, let me ask ya this: if the big hot shot makes so
damn much money, why do we live in a stinkin' dump? We barely
have a roof over our heads. What, am I stupid? Do I look like an
idiot to ya?"

"No."

"Scotty, could ya be a dear and rub some of this crap on my
legs?" she asks, widening her stance.

The "crap" was baby oil, and I never felt like I could say no, even
though all I ever wanted to say was no.

"I don't want to get my scout uniform oily."

"Then take it off."

"I'll be careful."

"You look sharp in that, soldier. Ahh, you're such a good listener;
if only you were forty years older I'd have my way with you. That's
right, honey, get it up in there; get those thighs good so mama don't
get glaucoma. That's it. Ahhhh."

If I had known any better, I'd have been creeped out by the
whole scenario, but I sensed it helped her to talk. She felt better by
getting things off her chest, and while I stood there nodding my
head to the same story over and over, in my mind I went away. I
went to cocktail parties where the host might be Batman or Oscar
the Grouch.

"Hey Oscar, I didn't know you were so tall," I'd say while
delicately sipping from a glass of Mountain Dew with an umbrella
tucked in it.

"That's 'cause they never let me out of the can! They don't want you to know I have legs; they think the kids will be freaked out," Oscar would retort while nibbling on a shrimp cocktail.

"That's silly of them. You have arms, why wouldn't you have legs?"

"So you wouldn't freak out if I stepped out of the can and started running around Sesame Street?"

"No. I'd freak out if you stepped out of the can and didn't have legs."

Oscar would pat me on the back. "Scott, you are so smart. They should make you mayor of Sesame Street."

It would go on and on like that while Helen stared into her glass.

"Sure I drink. I drink cause I have to. I drink—don't forget the feet, sweetie. The liquor's all I got left. I'm not happy about it; it's just a fact of life. Like the yellow piss stains in his underwear. But I'm not bitter. But he's at all the parties, bragging about his big six-figure Citibank job. Well then, why am I driving a '67 Pontiac to the Stop & Shop to get Food Club brand doughnuts? Ya want to know how that feels? It hurts. That's why I smoke so goddamn much. To cloud the pain. That's why I have yellow teeth."

"Uh huh," I'd say, spraying the oil on her feet, hoping I didn't have to rub it in.

"They match his underwear, the pompous bastard—sweet child, rub it in Helen's feet, would ya? People are always bitching to me to put out my cigarette. 'Put it out! Put it out!' I'll put it out all right, right in their faces." She exhales dramatically to illuminate her point. "'Smell that,' I say, 'That's fresh breath to me.' I don't want to smoke this much. As a matter of fact, I'm embarrassed by how much I smoke, one after another. When I'm lighting up a new one with the butt of the last, I tell people I'm lighting it for Carl. So I have yellow teeth. Why? Because I don't have a six-figure job to pay to have them whitened. He'll get his day, just ya wait."

The sad fact was, Carl had already relocated to Minneapolis and hadn't taken Helen with him. I overheard Mom talking about it at the beauty salon. Helen never mentioned it, nor did she ever alter her story, but you could see in her eyes that she knew he was gone and he wasn't coming back. She was just putting up a good fight. And as I stood there watching her, listening to a variation of the same story every week, I felt sorry for her, and that's why I cut through her yard. She needed someone to listen. It was my duty as a scout.

"So no, I'm not Cindy Crawford, I'm not Cher, but when I'm being fucked by the neighbor, I have worth. I feel pretty. I'm wanted. It's simple psychology. Can you understand that, son?"

"I'm sorry, Helen, I'm going to be late for scouts if I don't—"

"Am I proud of it? No. It's embarrassing to have to stand here with a drink in my hand, a cigarette in my mouth and tell ya that I get fucked by the neighbor because my six-figure of a husband can't get his dick hard when he stumbles home at five in the morning. Ya see how the third step is broken? Ya can guess who did that. And can he fix it? Hell no! Listen, Scottie, maybe ya could get a Cub Scout badge for fixing that. Could ya? Do ya think? Maybe they have a badge for helping out drunken old farts who are getting fucked over by their husbands."

"Ummmm … I'd have to check the scout manual."

"Every morning I say to myself, 'Watch the third step, Helen. Helen, you watch that third step.' But today, no. Flat on my ass. I forget. I can hear the neighbors laughing. 'There she is, drunk already this morning.' Well, that's it. Tonight I'm locking that door, and he's not stepping one foot inside this house; and tomorrow morning I'm serving him the papers. I can't wait to see the look on his six-figure face when he's served papers at his big six-figure Citibank job, with his fat gut hanging over his piss-stained underwear. He'll get his day. He'll get it."

She was at the age where she wasn't happy unless she was angry. Even when she was laughing, there was still bitterness in her eyes. Her vengeance story eventually faded and evolved into some other lonely story, or another tale about how someone wronged her in town.

One day she invited me into her home, saying she found something she wanted to show me. I had never been in her house before, and walking up the steps I wondered if this was a good idea. Would I ever make it out alive? I could probably outrun her, I thought, or at least push her over before she stabbed me or pulled the trigger. What if she poisoned my soup? There is no defending yourself against that.

The inside seemed smaller than it looked from the outside. It was musty, with a smell similar to that of my grandma's cellar on the farm. There were blankets covering the windows to prevent any chance of sunlight from entering. The living room was lit by three lamps that illuminated little more than the tables they sat on.

"They're in here," she said almost merrily as she stepped through a doorway that led to the kitchen.

I froze when I saw the black and white tile. It was the same tile that covered my grandparents' kitchen floor. That, coupled with the smell of must, brought a flash of a memory to when I was six or seven, sitting on the floor playing with the baby gosling that Grandpa brought in for me to play with. One of my favorite things in the world was playing with the baby geese. Grandma, however, didn't want them in the house, so when Grandpa heard her coming up from downstairs, he quickly shoved it under his cap. "Roy, did I hear a gosling down here?" she said coming into the kitchen. "Nope," he said, "you know the rules: no geese allowed in the house." And right on cue from under his cap came a *honk*.

"Roy, get that bird outside before it craps in the house."

Grandpa reached under his cap and said, "Whoops, I think it's too late."

"Do you want something to drink?" Helen asked me, yanking the fridge door, which resisted as if it hadn't been opened in years. There was nothing in there. Maybe a few stray items, but nothing to offer anyone to drink, at least no one of my age. "Beer?"

"No," I quickly responded.

Along with a few cartons of cigarettes, two black and white photos rested on the table. Her shaky hand reached out for one and handed it to me. "Take a look."

It was a classroom full of students posing for the camera and I could only assume she was one of the young girls behind a desk. She pointed to one and commented, "Pretty one, huh?"

"Yes, very pretty," I replied. I knew that was the only answer, but it happened to also be true. The young girl was sensational. She had dark, wavy hair that flipped up at the end, with a pale, sweet face that was accented with some dark lipstick. She was distinctly more attractive than the other girls. I looked up at Helen and then back down to the picture, finding it nearly impossible to believe that this was once her. "You were very beautiful, Helen. Still are," I quickly added.

"Oh, I was all right," she said, "but that's not me; that's your mother."

My chest hurt. How could I possibly have found my mom attractive? "No. That can't be Mom," I demanded.

"Why not?"

"She's pretty." It was the first time I had seen my mom looking like someone other than my mom.

"Well, it most certainly is. That's me," she said pointing to the teacher.

I looked up at her again. "You were my mom's teacher?"

She sat down to light up another cigarette. "Yep. We moved to Ellendale so I could teach. Carl golfed and sold fertilizer for a company out of Minneapolis."

Now I was intrigued. "Did she get any Ds?" I asked, hopeful.

"Nope. Smart as a whip, she was."

"So you taught my dad, too? 'Cause they went to school together."

She picked up the other photo, which was a shot of my dad standing behind a science-type table. His eyes were crossed as he pretended a test tube was stuck on his finger. I laughed. "Yeah, that's him. Did he get any Ds?" I asked.

"Sorry."

I sat there and stared at the photos while she sat silently smoking. It was unsettling to see my parents so young; it meant someday I was going to look like they looked. Helen's house was still and deeply quiet with so many blankets covering the windows. I could hear the paper on her cigarette crackle as it burned its way toward the filter. I eventually let the photos come to rest once again upon the table, but still said nothing. It was so comforting to sit silently with my friend Helen, who taught my parents and obviously knew a world more than I did about them.

Helen finally sputtered, "I'm surprised they got married."

"What?" I remember my heart pain after Helen said that. It scared me. I thought perhaps they weren't meant for each other, or worse, that I was a mistake and forced their hand in marriage.

"Your grandfather was a son-of-a-bitch," she continued. "It can't be easy being the son of the local minister. Especially those damn Methodists. Your dad wasn't allowed to do a thing the other kids could do."

"Grandpa was strict?"

"Strict? I should say so. Of course, being a teacher, I knew everything that was going on with the kids. I heard every whispered story and read every note that was carelessly left behind. There was more drama in those kids' lives than any Hollywood soap opera could dream up." She laughed to herself from the thought of it. "Your poor mom suffered. They'd been dating their entire junior year, and come prom time, your father wasn't allowed to go! Can you believe it?"

I wasn't sure at the time what a prom was, much less the importance of it. But from the excitement Helen was exuding, I concluded it was a big deal for a girl not to go.

"At that time Carl and I were attending your grandfather's church on a regular basis, and I tell you what: every Sunday walking past him during the handshaking procession I wanted to knee him in the balls. *How dare you not let your son go to prom, for Christ's sake?* Don't worry, I said nothing, but it boiled my blood. Finally, a year later, when your sweet mother was nominated for homecoming queen her senior year, your father was allowed to go to the dance. I believe your grandmother had something to do with that. She was the strong silent type, never had much to say, but when she did, I think your grandfather listened.

Your mother couldn't have been happier, you understand. Elated! Until the day of the dance when …" Helen took a long dramatic drag from her cigarette. A deep drag, all the way to the filter, and then snuffed it out in a vacant can of Budweiser. "Hold tight, my bladder's knockin' on the door."

As Helen made her way into the bathroom, I looked back down at the photo of my mom. Even though I was only ten, I could still recognize that she was something special. I felt so proud thinking about her hearing the announcement at school that she was voted to become homecoming queen. I imagined all her friends hugging her, and the all the boys jealous of my dad. In the photo she sat straight up in her seat, poised. She looked so happy, so full of potential.

"Shit!" Helen blurted from behind the sliding bathroom door that was just off the kitchen. "Are there any napkins out there?"

I spotted a pile near the refrigerator. "Yes."

"Be a doll and slide one through the crack, would you?"

The crack was actually a wide gap, which I regret revealed more of Helen than I wanted it to. She wedged her hand through like an old withered tree root protruding from the ground. I handed her the napkin and shuffled back to my chair.

"I got something else for you!" she punctuated with the flush of the toilet.

I sat there staring at the door, frightened that whatever it might be was coming from within the bathroom. It didn't. She pulled an old, wrinkled piece of brown paper bag from within the pages of a large book that was standing in for a missing leg under her living room chair.

"Here, read this," she said, handing me the bag. "It was a note from your dad that I confiscated from your mother during math. I told her she could have it back after class, but she never came for it. Too embarrassed, I guess. I only took it 'cause I knew it would be juicy. It was the day of the homecoming dance and for some strange reason she was quite glum."

I gently pinched the note between two fingers and unfolded it like an important document that held the secret identity of the tooth fairy.

"Sure you don't want a beer?" she asked, once again making her way to the fridge. "Have a beer."

I loved the feeling of adulthood that filled me when I was with Helen. I had a secret document and now was being offered booze. "No, thanks." I continued to stare at the words, marveling at my father's neat penmanship. He wrote in a very curly cursive. Just as I was about to begin, Helen snatched it from my hands.

"It'll go quicker if I do it. There are some big words in there." She flattened it out on the hard table and then held it up and out the full length of her arm. "You might be able to see it better, but I can read it better." She cleared her throat and began: "To my dear queen. I have never been more excited than the day my father allowed me to accompany you to the homecoming dance. As a minister, it was a difficult thing for him to permit, but I guess he figured it would be more difficult for me, given how much I adore you. Over the last week, however, my father has received a great number of calls from the congregation protesting his decision to let his son attend the homecoming dance. It's been hard on him. He tried keeping it from me, but I overheard one of the calls last night. Out of respect for my father and his position in the church, I'm going to have to cancel our date for the dance. This hurts me a great deal as I imagine it does you. Please understand and find it in your heart to forgive me. On the bright side, you can take pleasure in gloating that you were crowned queen but I wasn't crowned king. It came as no surprise to me, as you are clearly the good-looking one in this relationship. I will be thinking about you tonight and trust you will have a majestic time. Yours always, Richard."

With that, Helen slammed the note down on the table like she had a royal flush. The note just sat there, filling the dramatic silence that it had created. Helen lit up another cigarette as I dangled my feet off the edge of the chair, wondering if my mother was still sad about not going with Dad to the dance. At that time I didn't care about stupid dances, but I was pretty sure that a girl who was crowned the high school queen would take interest. Was there ever a time in the history of high school that a queen didn't have a date to the homecoming dance?

"Can you believe that shit!" Helen protested. "I tell you what, that was the last time I stepped foot in the Methodist church. You have another think coming if you think I was going to go sit among those idiots ever again. Hell no! God wasn't getting any more of my business if he thought he could mess around with the joy of one of my students. Unbelievable. Your mother was crushed, to say the least. Devastated."

I thought to myself, *Tonight I'm going to ask my parents at dinner all about their childhood, to see if there are any more interesting stories I can dig up.* I never did, of course. But I do remember staring back and forth at each of their faces, as they slurped up bowls of oyster stew, imagining them as those high school kids I saw in the photos earlier that day.

Helen folded the note. "I plan to give these pictures and the note to your parents for their fifteenth wedding anniversary."

"They'll like that," I offered.

"Well, should we?" Helen asked, indicating that show-and-tell was over and we should return to the outside.

"Wait, a minute. So they never got to go to dances or anything together? How did they ever get to be married, then?"

Helen took a deep contemplative breath and looked up to the ceiling. "Oh ... well, your father eventually resolved things with your grandfather, and they went to the prom their senior year. At that time I started chaperoning the dances after Pat Tuttle broke her hip. Once you break a hip you are never the same. I remember your poor father, who had never been to a dance, didn't know what he was doing. Your mother showed him the steps to all the dances. She was very patient. I think they fell in love that night. It wasn't long after that that your father proposed. Well, it wasn't a formal proposal as such. I remember he came running into my classroom, all sweaty, threw a small cardboard box at your mother and said, 'It just came in the mail at lunch.' Well, class couldn't continue until she opened the box, I knew that, and so she did. And by God if it wasn't a diamond ring."

"He ordered a wedding ring in the mail? I thought you got them at the mall?"

"Not your father. He was a character. Played by a different way of thinking."

Helen and I found our way back into the bright sunlight of the afternoon. I was late for Dwight's, so I took off running, giddy with delight that I had a secret.

I didn't collect a scout badge for my moments with Helen, but what I did get was even greater: stories of my parents' love. The stories continued. Every week Helen remembered something new, and I was more than willing to drink it in for the price of an oil rubdown. Ironically, a year before my parents' divorce, I felt a greater appreciation for their relationship. A deeper coziness came when my parents tucked me into bed those nights. As they would walk out of my room, silhouetted in the light of the hallway, I could easily imagine their arms conservatively draped over one another's shoulders as the homecoming queen taught the minister's son to waltz.

The aroma of the Hendersons' jasmine wafts over from across the street, pulling my thoughts away from Helen and back to the empty pit, which will soon be a warehouse full of caskets and patio furniture. I wonder, *Will Helen's casket come from here when her time comes?* Then I realize it's time to go. In the few moments of standing in the cool air, my joints have stiffened and temporarily misfire as I make my way back down the wet sidewalk to my car, a shake of my hair and one last cleansing breath of jasmine to take with me.

SEVENTH STREET
Gestalt Therapy

I pull into the Wooden Nickel bar parking lot to dump some trash in the can that sits on the corner of Seventh Street. As usual, the can is spilling over with empty beer bottles from the night before. The Wooden Nickel is an old brick structure that looks as if it may have been a bank, as it still has a drive-up window where you can purchase off-sale liquor. Strangely enough, many guys like to buy a twelve-pack, park, and then sit on their tailgates and pound a few back with their buddies. I open my window and drop the small bag of trash next to the can.

I have two memories of this bar; one is a funny memory and the other sparks a measure of pain. For the first nine years of my life, it's where my father drank, until the alcohol systematically tore apart the fabric of our family.

I've been electrocuted by a cattle fence, and even had bones broken, but one simple phrase my mother said to me is without question the most painful moment in my life to date, one of those moments where time appeared to stand still. I was nine years old, and my mother and I were on the way back into town after having taken a trip to my grandparents'—without my father.

At that time we lived in the west part of the town, near the highway you would take to travel across the state. Once we exited the highway after a trip back home from the farm, it was no more than a few blocks before we pulled into the driveway of the single-story duplex where I grew up.

"You missed the turn, Mom, aren't we going home?" I asked suspiciously, after a weekend full of whispered statements and walking in on heavy conversations between my mother and her parents. I was sitting in the backseat for some reason, possibly out of habit, and remember looking out the passenger window and then the back window as we drove past the turn to our home. And with a haunting, emotional timbre that belied its casual delivery, she said the words: "No. We're never going home again." I was nine when I heard those words. The foundation of my soul had never been shaken to the point of cracking before. The temperature outside the car, the temperature inside, the smells, the images, the sounds of cars going past, the color of the trees—the vividness and exactness of that moment have yet to diminish in my mind some fourteen years later.

We spent the next two weeks living in a spare bedroom at the home of a friend of my parents. It was a chilling and disorienting fourteen days. I remember sitting every night after school in a cold basement watching television, while behind the scenes I sensed my world was being turned upside down. The next thing I knew, we moved into our new condo: three bedrooms, an unfinished basement, one garage, and zero fathers. I secretly checked the closets in the hope of finding his suits hanging there waiting for his arrival. Nothing. No shoes, no *Sports Illustrated* magazines, no shaving cream, no slippers, no robe, no hats, no father.

A few months later my father was excused from his job at the university and went off the radar. I was never told exactly what was going on, but had overheard enough from the crack below my bedroom door to piece together that Mom would be on her own financially. Within the year, Dad went into a rehabilitation center in Jamestown. Toward the end of his treatment he asked my mom if the two of us would come to family day at the treatment center. She agreed, and I was excited, because we were going to do something as a family again, which hadn't happened in a long time. Despite the fact that Todd was not going along because he was apparently not old enough, I remained excited because maybe this was the road back to being a family unit again. But what I thought was going to be a day of fun and games and water-balloons, turned out to be a day of Gestalt therapy in a public arena. This was a whole different kind of fun.

My family sat on brown folding chairs in a small circle with four other "dysfunctional" families surrounding us in a larger circle. This was called a *fish bowl*. My mother and father had been fielding painful questions for a half hour when the counselor turned to me for the final leg of her breaking-people-down tour. She asked what made me angry about my father's drinking.

Oh, I don't know. He kept hogging all the alcohol? Ummm, let's see, it broke up the only family I would ever have in this lifetime? Maybe the fact that I would spend the next thirteen years being ashamed of having a single parent and would lie about it to anyone I met?

In the moment, however, all I could do was stare at the gray carpeting, thinking how unfair it was that I had been put in this position. What did I do wrong? Was I not a good son? Did I fail in my job of being the firstborn? Is this about me still wetting the bed? Had it made him feel like such a failure as a father that he had to start drinking? I thought about the basketball game I had to miss because of this "family day" and wondered what excuse my mother gave the coach. I'll bet she told the truth. I thought about quitting the team, so I wouldn't have to face the coach again, or maybe he would feel sorry for me and give me more court time. Did I want more court time? By that point in my life it wasn't too difficult to figure out that I wasn't designed for sports and was doing it only because my father had been a huge athlete.

I used to love looking at my father's high school yearbooks, admiring all the different athletic teams he was on. I wanted to be just like the guy in the pictures; the only thing I was missing was the athleticism. But to this point in my life, I didn't know any better. The divorce marked the beginning of a lifetime of me living my life for other people, trying to be what I thought others wanted me to be so that the world would go on smoothly without any further disruptions. It's unnatural, and my system has been subconsciously fighting against it for years. The results manifest themselves in bouts of misdirected anger, sudden feelings of worthlessness, or a limited tolerance that drives me to rage when a family at the Olive Green asks me for limes instead of lemons.

Driving out of town today is my first big, conscious step *against* trying to please everyone, and it's difficult not to give in. Every part of me wants to turn the car around, apply for a managerial position at Target, marry my high school girlfriend, move into the apartment complex across the street from Mom, and call it a life.

The therapist cleared her throat and addressed me once again. "Scott, can you tell me what made you angry about your father's drinking?"

I looked out the corner of my eye to see if anyone was looking at me. Of course everyone was. They were waiting for me to answer the question, which had been asked twice, and I was miles from answering. Not to say I didn't have answers. No, I had plenty of fucking answers. The answers were churning in my stomach and making my heart pound faster than it ever had before. The answers scared me, and I had started trembling at the prospect of my father hearing them. They weren't answers he'd be pleased with, and hearing them in front of complete strangers would be humiliating. The gray carpeting looked so comforting. I couldn't take my eyes off it. I wanted to curl up on it under my chair. Once under there, I would dig myself deep into its fibers, and in my mind, go to a *real* family day—like Christmas.

When I was younger we spent holidays on the farm, and every Christmas Eve was present time for us. I always felt sorry for the poor saps whose parents made them wait until Christmas morning. Right after dinner I was the first in the living room and settled, Indian style, on the shag carpeting. While the adults took their sweet time getting into their adult chairs, I would rummage under the tree to find the present I wanted to open first. Dad, being somewhat of a child himself, would sidle up next to me on the floor wearing a cockeyed Santa's beard and a baseball cap. Having not only athletic talent but also somewhat of an artistic touch flowing in him, my mother always put him in charge of wrapping presents. His big stunt was to intentionally leave off the nametags so that if at any point the evening became dull, he could, à la Jerry Lewis, become completely befuddled as to which present went to whom.

"Umm … let me see … Here you go, Scotty. No wait, that's Grandpa's I think; or is it Mom's? No, I remember; the red one is yours and the … Hold on, what's that yellow one doing under there? I didn't wrap that. Or did I? Now I know for certain the blue one is mine."

That was Dad's favorite part of Christmas, and the more I got frustrated with him, the more cross-eyed and confused he pretended to be. My mother and grandparents laughed until they nearly slid out of their chairs. But Dad never broke character; he kept a straight face the entire time. One year he mischievously let me open one of my grandmother's presents, which turned out to be a Playtex support bra. The moment my face dropped, he busted out laughing with the rest of them. I quickly recovered and acted as if it was the best present I'd ever opened. Every year after that, we chuckled over the pictures of me walking around in Grandma's white bra.

It's that kind of happy memory I was thinking about when Mom mentioned family day—not sitting on a cold metal chair with a counselor staring me down, waiting for an answer.

Once I realized I was going to have to say or do something to pacify this counselor, the tears started to fall. They fell fast and hard onto my light blue shirt. The fact that Mom made me put on a dress shirt that morning should have been an indication that I wasn't going to be playing dodgeball or competing in any potato sack races. Long sleeve, light blue button-downs are not designed for fun; they're for church or other emotional tortures. My breathing had become labored; I was gasping for breath. I wanted so badly to wipe my sleeve across the stream of snot that was threatening to jump my upper lip and rappel to my lap. I was hoping at that point that they would realize I was incapacitated and move on to the next family.

"Can you look at your father and tell him what made you mad about his drinking?"

Is she kidding? I thought. *Look at my father? Raise my head and look my father in the eyes? I had never looked him in the eyes before. What made her think this would be the time I might start?*

I shook my head: *No.*

This time the counselor used her stern tone. "I need you to look at your father and tell him what made you mad about his drinking." She meant business. I could feel the dynamic in the room change, and hear people shift nervously in their metal folding chairs. They felt bad for me. I heard a mother behind me let out an exasperated sigh as if to say, "Just leave the poor child alone, already. Look at him, for Christ's sake, you've done enough damage."

Her sigh gave me strength. I slowly brought my head up. I saw my dad's hand resting on his leg, kneading a fistful of Kleenex. Nervous. I moved my focus up, and there he was: my father, sobbing and looking down at his lap. There were no eyes to make contact with. This strong man was crying harder than I was. He had been defeated. He was helpless and at a place in life he certainly never could have envisioned, placed on a public pedestal with a wife and a son expressing their disappointment in him.

"Tell him how his drinking made you feel, Scott," she said, wanting me to destroy him further.

I felt like telling her to fuck off. I wanted to jump out of my chair and kick her in the glasses, and like the wrestlers on television, smash my folding chair over her head until blood streamed down her face. I was so angry with her for doing this to my family. *She* was to blame, not my father.

"Scott?" she said, urging me on.

I couldn't. I didn't want to hurt him anymore. I knew what she wanted me to say. She wanted me to talk about the fighting, or how he missed my basketball games and my band concerts. How I was embarrassed to bring friends home because I was afraid he would be drunk and start yelling. Or how all I wanted was to have a regular family who had breakfast together in the morning and went on vacations. Or how my gut turned over on itself when I would find a tiny bit of scotch at the bottom of a glass hidden behind his chair, and would empty it in a hurry so Mom wouldn't find it. Or how every time—

"Scott, it's okay. Simply tell him what bothered you."

I looked first to my mother who gave me a gentle, tearstained smile of support and then back to my father who still couldn't look up, and I decided our session was over. Our family had suffered enough and we didn't need any more.

"Ice cubes," I blurted out.

"What about the ice cubes?"

I shrugged. "They were a little bit loud. In his glass. They clinked in his glass when he was drinking at night, and sometimes it kept me awake."

I gave the counselor a determined look and said firmly, "That's all."

She held my eyes for a long moment and finally retired her reproach. "Thank you." Then she looked to my father and asked if he would like to give me a hug. The word *hug* had barely left her lips when he fell forward to his knees and wobbled toward me like an injured animal. He wrapped both arms around me tightly, with his head resting vulnerably on my stomach like a baby. My mother willfully rose from her brown chair and held both of us tightly, and there on the gray carpeting, we wept away our anger and resentment. We wept until our hearts felt peace once again.

The Wooden Nickel is also where Melvin Knutson put on his karaoke tribute to Neil Diamond, appropriately titled "Love on the Rocks." Across the top of the poster: "Love on the Rocks. A tribute to Neil Diamond. At the Wooden Nickel, May 10th at 8:00 a.m. sharp." Yeah, it was an unfortunate misprint—he meant "p.m." But in Fargo it doesn't really matter. You don't need a poster; all you need is the ladies of the beauty salon to know, and they did.

Melvin went to high school with me. He was an overweight mechanic who worked at the Texaco station, and just between you and me, Melvin was a little ... funny. *Funny* is my mother's word for "homosexual." "He's a little funny, isn't he?" she'd say. Unless it was a female, in which case she called them *lezzies*. Anyone who was a little "off" made her suspicious that they were homosexuals. Unless they were so "off" that they were mentally handicapped; then she just called them *goofy*.

Everybody knew Melvin was funny, but it's not the type of thing you discuss in Fargo; it's the type of thing you deny in order to deal. So, if you're an automobile owner and the only mechanic in town is gay, by God, you deny it. Or you end up riding your bike. We're not prejudiced, and it's not that we don't like the gays ... or blacks or Jews or Asians. We're just not comfortable around them. We're not very good with the unfamiliar. We like what we know. We like cheddar, Swiss, and Velveeta, but not Brie. Mom would need to wear one of Ginger's ball gags if she went to a big city because she innocently calls black people "nigroos" and Asian people "Orientals."

Melvin pulled out all the stops that night. For years he put a little money aside from each check. He ordered a special black sequined jumpsuit from a catalog that he got when he was in Vegas. He bought a karaoke machine from Target with twelve of Neil Diamond's top hits, and on Friday night at the Wooden Nickel, the karaoke machine was lit up like a Christmas tree. Melvin became Neil Diamond.

The bar was packed because they all wanted to support their local mechanic, thereby maintaining a place on the car lift if their vehicle should happen to break down. All of us from his high school class were in attendance as well. The Wooden Nickel, as with most bars in Fargo, was the kind of place anyone of any age could hang out.

I feared we were in for a long evening when Melvin began using his fingers to count out the beats in the intro to his first song. My fears were confirmed upon hearing the first note. It was in a key that Neil had never intended, a key unfamiliar to humans.

"Haaaaands, touching haaaaands. Reaching ooooout. Touching meeeeee. Touching yooooou. Sweeeeet Caroliiiiiiiine. Bum, bum, bummmmm."

The "bums" are the best part of the song because they're the part the crowd gets to join in. Nobody sang the "bums." I think everyone was afraid it would throw him off the beat, which was only occasionally maintained.

"Good times never seemed so good."

The lyrics didn't exactly reflect the mood of the bar. These "good times" were making our ears all a little uncomfortable.

And then.

The music stopped. Melvin looked over at the machine. We all looked over at the machine. No more Christmas tree. It was dead.

But there was a look in his eye like Neil had taken over his soul and he was saying, "Ah, fuck it, kid." And Melvin continued on. Unfortunately, Neil's sense of pitch had evaded Melvin's soul.

"I've been inclined ... to believe there never would ..."

The pitch kept going down and down until he could no longer sing that low and he abruptly ended the song. Despite his mechanical genius with combustible engines, he couldn't manage to fix the karaoke machine between songs.

Melvin finished the hour and a half show *a cappella*. And because of the sparkly sequined jumpsuit, my mom thought it was the best piece of theatre she'd ever seen.

Immediately after my father's stint in rehab, Mom told me that my dad was going to be staying with us until he could find a job and get back on his feet. I had always held on to the hope that my parents would some day get back together, and this seemed like a step in the right direction. Since he was going to be staying in our unfinished basement, I spent hours making it livable before his arrival. I decided a fort might make the musty, dank cement more of a home, so I laid a piece of foam under the Ping-Pong table and hung blankets to create four walls.

Despite only being ten years old, something inside of me must have understood just how humiliating it was for a grown man, a college graduate, and most importantly, a father, to swallow his pride and ask his ex-wife if he could sleep under the Ping-Pong table in her basement.

Something in rehab must have stuck, because he handled this difficult valley with optimism and integrity. He loved the fort and continued on and on about how it was better than the time he stayed at Caesar's Palace in Vegas. Each night before bed we would play a few games of Ping-Pong while Mom sat on the steps and kept score. It was all I had ever wanted in a family.

Since we didn't have an extra alarm clock, he put me in charge of getting him up every morning. The sense of responsibility brought me such a thrill that often I couldn't sleep at night from the anticipation. I remember repeatedly rolling over in my bed to check the clock, anxious that the alarm hadn't gone off and I was late for my duty. Dad must have sensed my excitement for the job, and protected it at all costs, because one morning while sprinting toward the stairs, I noticed there was coffee already percolating in the kitchen, which could only mean he had already been up, as my mother doesn't drink coffee.

Upon reaching the bottom of the wooden staircase, I was shocked to find him still asleep on the foam mattress. After tapping him on the shoulder and pulling down the covers I noticed he was already dressed. He played the role of groggy like he had just gotten up, but I knew he had crawled back in after hearing my approaching footsteps.

My efforts to patch our little family back together with a piece of foam and some blanket walls failed. After two weeks my dad secured a job selling World Book Encyclopedias door-to-door, and after a month, he moved out. I kept the blankets in place just in case, and Mom even let me sleep in the fort for a couple days after he left, but he wasn't coming back.

As I laid on the foam bed staring up at the bottom of the Ping-Pong table, I thought of all the things I could have done to make the fort better, which perhaps would have encouraged him to stay longer; a picture of our family would have been comforting, and flowers could have overpowered the musty odors that still lingered in the cracks of the cement floor.

The fact is, the alcohol isn't the reason why my parents divorced; it's the excuse. The reason is simple. They were raised in the small town Ellendale, population maybe three hundred people at the time, went to the same high school, and got married because they were the most likely pairing in their senior class. This is a sad phenomenon that happens not only in small towns in America, but many cultures across the world. Both my parents to this day claim they didn't think they were right for one another, but resigned to parental and social pressures. The only reason their marriage may have lasted as long as it did was because they kept themselves too busy to notice they were falling out of love, if in fact, they were ever *in* love.

They both acquired teaching degrees from the nearest college, and immediately following, bounced around a few small towns in the tri-state area teaching high school. Dad, being a natural athlete, taught physical education, and because the schools were so small, coached most of the team sports. Mom taught English and kept herself busy with any after school activity group that wasn't athletic.

Months before I was ready to pop out of the womb, Dad accepted a nine-to-five job as the director of the athletic department at the university in Fargo. Mom stayed home, and life slowed down for both of them. Things became routine, and they were finally confronted with the fact that they were married to people that they didn't love, yet had a child on the way. In classic Midwestern style, my mother internalized her objections and put on a happy face, my father turned to the bottle, and ten years later we're all sitting on brown folding chairs in a fish bowl.

Mom is still searching for the right man, and I imagine this will intensify now that I'm leaving. Three years later, my father married a wonderful woman whom Todd and I both really love. Dad went on to get his doctorate—in psychology, of all things—and is now forcing *other* families to work out *their* issues in the fish bowl. He hasn't touched a drop of alcohol in eleven years.

As for me, I like bourbon. Neat. Because every time I hear ice clinking in a glass, I think of "family day," and of my father kneading those goddamn Kleenexes in his fist. And how I was naïve enough to believe family day meant fun and games and water balloons.

SIXTH STREET
Potty Pal

Pulling out of the Wooden Nickel, I take a right on to Sheyenne Street and immediately past the five-unit strip mall that occupies the entire plot of land between Sixth and Fifth Streets. I notice for the first time that many of the stores which were apart of my childhood are now gone. The National Counsel for Lutheran Women's Thrift Store ... gone. It was where Mom bought all my school clothes. While other kids were at home matching Granimals tags, I was at home deciding if I'd get my ass kicked less wearing polka dots or paisley.

Next to that was the OK Hardware store; not great, but okay. But not okay enough to stay in business, apparently, since it's now a Laundromat.

Then there's what remains of the Clip & Curl beauty salon, which was run by Frances Cermack, my mother's best friend, who had her stylist's license revoked and now runs an illegal salon out of her kitchen. Frances doesn't cut hair as much as she teases it. So the shorter you want it, the higher it must go. She used hairspray like a barber used scissors. Frances was also a big smoker. She was the human personification of Andy Capp; you never saw her without a Benson & Hedges dangling from her lip. She never touched the cigarette once she lit it. Ashes just fell freely to the linoleum, and when she was done, she'd simply spit the butt to the floor and step on it.

When the technique of perming hair made its way to Fargo, the ladies went crazy. They'd get a perm, and go back the next week and get another, piling one perm on top of the other. Then one year Mom decided her sons would look good with perms. We didn't. We looked like her. It was a horrifying process with a roomful of spectators. Since the salon was in her kitchen, Frances didn't have one of those industrial hooded hair dryers. Instead, she had this rinky-dink shower cap with a big hose coming out of it that puffed up like a bag of Jiffy Pop.

It was a Wednesday. I know, because every Tuesday, to this day, my mother gets her hair done. She gets it done, mind you, from 10:00 a.m. to 4:00 p.m. Now you may be thinking: *Six hours. Isn't that a long time?* Yes, it is a long time—suspiciously long when you consider my mother doesn't look that much different coming out than she does going in, except her hair is slightly higher, closer to God. It wasn't referred to as the "Blather Salon" for nothing.

It was the third Tuesday of the month, which meant Nita Edilberg had driven over from Bergen County because, apparently, they don't have a kitchen that does hair. When she wasn't around she was referred to as Nita Evil-berg. The "Evil" isn't added because she likes to jump over things with a motorcycle, but because, as Frances likes to put it:

"She's an evil bitch."

Nita was hell-bent for pity that afternoon and droned on and on about how she might have to get her teeth capped, but she can't afford the dentist who's all the way in Minneapolis, and how her car won't make it there even if she could afford it. On and on. She just put five hundred dollars into her car and it barely gets her into Fargo for bingo once a week. In Fargo they don't brag about accomplishments, so they try to outdo one another's suffering, much in the same way your grandfather would brag to you about how he had to walk seven miles to school in the snow—backward.

Apparently Nita's tales had been paraded under my mother's nose one too many times, and she started to grow angry, knowing perfectly well her family was equally as miserable as Nita's. Tired of having her misery minimized and overshadowed month after month, my mother finally snapped.

"Nita, I don't mean to get nasty, but I'll have you know that twice a night I get out of bed to change my son's urine-soaked sheets. That's right, he's thirteen and still wets the bed; and we've been to every doctor in the Cass County and they don't know what's wrong with him. As far as we know, he'll wet the bed for the rest of his life. So there, I said it."

And on that, she stormed out, with pride on her chest and curlers on her head, rendering Frances's kitchen silent for the first time ever. The silence was eventually broken, and it didn't take long for the scuttlebutt weed to weave its way through the grapevine of our small town.

"He doesn't seem like a bed wetter."

"What a shame."

"Intentionally?"

"Is it contagious?"

"He was such a good little trumpet player."

"Marge, he's not dead."

"Might as well be."

That evening Mom made brownies, which made me suspicious, because it was the only weapon she ever deployed to right her wrongs.

"Scott, listen," she said, "I sort of made a boo-boo. I told Nita and the girls that you were still wetting the bed. Here, have a brownie."

"You what?"

"Mmmmm ... they're moist. Oh, don't look at me like that. They probably won't think twice about it."

"You call that a boo-boo?"

"Have two."

And there it was. The beginning of the end of my life.

Most mornings I had a bounce in my step on the way to school. And why not? I was thirteen, with a blemish-free face that I'm positive was the talk of the hallways. Things were going well. I was the third-string quarterback, played second-chair trumpet and was going steady with Gretchen, the second-best-looking wrestling cheerleader. Not bad for a kid with two fake front teeth. But that Wednesday the bounce was replaced with a slink. What would I say? "My mom's an idiot." "My mom has hot flashes which melt her brain." "She eats a lot of fried food." Crap! It didn't matter; they wouldn't believe anything I said anyway.

By second period I was still the talk of the hallways, of course. By third period, Gretchen, the second-best-looking wrestling cheerleader, cornered me in the library with a look that told me her mother had just gotten her hair heightened. She handed me back the ID bracelet I had purchased for her at Walgreens not two weeks ago and told me she needed to start focusing more on her studies if she was ever going to make it as a beautician. "Focus on my studies" was the junior high equivalent of "It's not you, it's me."

I sat alone at the lunch table wondering why my best friend Tyler just cancelled his plans to sleep over for the weekend. Then it hit me: bunk beds. He had no interest in spending the night because the idea of sleeping on the bottom bunk suddenly provided too great a risk, what with seepage and all. An obvious choice would have been for me to sleep on the bottom bunk, but this would have entailed him sleeping on the mattress I used the night before. It was a lose-lose situation.

After a couple of days, the talking in the hallways turned to pointing and giggling. So my mother, noticing my sustained bout of depression, embarked on a solution. She invested in the Potty Pal, a machine that would hopefully cure my problem and maybe relieve a little of her guilt. And when I say "invested," I mean purchased with her collection of S&H Green Stamps, perhaps one of the last items purchased before the death of the stamp. My mother was convinced the Potty Pal would cure my problem. I was convinced that no burden assigned to me by God was going to be cured by a machine that came with a free set of steak knives. It was certainly not going to win back the heart of the second-best-looking girl in school.

The creature was a little white box, a light, a siren, no instructions, and two wires that clipped onto a flat piece of—oh, I don't know … metal?—which was to be placed just under the fitted sheet that the victim would lie on. Glued to the upper left hand corner was a tiny ceramic bear wearing a large white diaper and a smile that seemed to be asking, "Won't ya be my pal?" A big, black, thick, electrical cord that plugged into a 210-volt industrial outlet, which no home would possess, powered the entire device. So my mother asked Crazy Kluger, a loathsome old man who ran a Harley Davidson repair shop out of his garage next door to ours, if she could string an extension cord to his garage.

Kluger was a Vietnam vet, and the type of guy you thought twice about borrowing a cup of sugar from unless you had an hour available to hear the latest version of how he lost an eye in the war. The neighborhood kids called him Crazy Kluger because every time they ran past, he yelled out, "I got your backs." He drew purpose from life by trying to keep the neighborhood free from enemy attacks. As I recall, our neighborhood was never at war; nonetheless, he built a six-foot tall guard chair from which he held post every night. Nobody ever complained because it was a form of free security, and he had yet to open fire on a stray cat that he might have mistaken for Vietcong.

My first slumber party with the bear was a school night, so bedtime was ten o'clock sharp. I remember my room felt cold and clinical, like a clinic in which people give blood or urinate into cups, or in my case, into an electrical outlet. I was nervous yet filled with relief at the prospect of never wetting the bed again. Just outside my window I heard Crazy Kluger whistling a tune, perched on his security tower.

Anticipation of an alarm going off in the middle of the night prevented me from any kind of sound sleep for many days. In fact, I slept so lightly that when I felt pressure on my bladder I immediately woke up. But one morning about four in the morning, the fear of God was sent through every nerve ending in my body. The Potty Pal was at full attention. The sound was deafening and the light blinding. I had no idea where or who I was.

I learned later that the alarm evidently had volume enough to send Kluger backward over his chair and flat to the ground. He must have thought we were under enemy attack, because through his homemade loudspeaker he was yelling, "Incoming! Incoming!" This woke the entire neighborhood and put them in my backyard, just outside my bedroom window. My mother, unable to detect the sound source and having forgotten about the machine, had run outside to see what the trouble was.

I was so startled that I rolled off the top bunk, got my head caught in the wires, and was now being strangled by the very machine that alleged to be my pal. My fall must have pulled the plug because the room had finally gone silent. All that remained was the ringing in my ears and the sound of my mom's revelation outside my bedroom window: "Oh yeah, that must have been my son's bedwetting machine. Never mind, sorry about that, you can all go back to bed now. Back to bed; sorry. Good night."

Like a loose tooth, I dangled helplessly in both utter humiliation and wet pajamas, pondering the questions that would inevitably be brought up next week in Frances Cermack's kitchen.

"So he actually pees on the machine?"

"Isn't it dangerous?"

"Do they make a quieter version?"

"Oh really, free steak knives?"

"Have you heard him play the trumpet? Isn't he just marvelous?"

That was the last of the Potty Pal. The truth is that I don't recall my problem stopping so much as it seems to have just slowly faded away. At first, it was a couple days without an accident, then a week, two weeks, eventually the intervals of time just kept getting longer and longer. Now my biggest fear is that the Potty Pal shocked my system, and I'm merely in the middle of one ludicrously long interval that will end the night of my honeymoon.

FIFTH STREET
Come to Jesus

Driving past the Walgreens I can see a glint of glare from a few of the trailers that sit in the trailer court directly behind it. This is where my "slightly simple" uncle Dwight lives. Dwight's trailer is where I would go after school and wait for Mom to get off work from the restaurant. I did this from third grade to sixth grade.

Dwight is a walking charcoal caricature with more fingers on one hand than teeth. He's what children across America dress up like on Halloween. He's a stay-at-home mechanic with the parenting skills of a welding torch. Surprising as it may seem, Dwight is not always on the cutting edge of fashion, unless you think camouflage is cutting edge. Dwight does. And he often says out loud and in public, "Camouflage is the fabric of our lives." Not understanding the difference between a fabric and a pattern, he continues to show his Southern influence. Everything is camouflage with him: boots, caps, jackets, gloves, and socks. At any time Dwight can stand perfectly still, he'll completely disappear into the background unless he's at the carnival. He even has a camouflage wallet, which makes you wonder: *Aren't there some things you just don't want to have blend into the ground?*

If you're residing in the western side of town, the last place you want to live is near the river. Dwight and his family reside not just in a trailer, but in a trailer that teeters on the banks of the Sheyenne River—which floods every year without fail. And every year following the damage, he proudly boasts, "We're gonna rebuild!" I'm not sure what that means when you live in a trailer, but he says it nonetheless. Perhaps it simply means he's going to replace the furniture and repanel the walls. Flood restoration has become almost a hobby for him. Some people plant a garden in the spring. Dwight "rebuilds."

One can't help but wonder if Dwight realizes his house is on wheels and could conveniently move it in the opposite direction of the rising water. Dwight appears to treat the yearly devastation like a vacation getaway. It provides him and his family with a completely different surrounding, as they get to stay in a motel. They stay at the Lucky 7 just off I–94. The name has nothing to do with gambling. In fact, the closest you can come to gambling there is *not* sliding a quarter into the condom machine.

Dwight's family never makes the move to safety until the last minute, when they have no choice but to climb off the roof and into their boat. Dwight has always fancied himself to be a James Bond of sorts, and with that, loves to push things to a dangerous level, be it with a Skil saw, riding lawn mower, or raging rivers. With an ounce of forethought, most of these precarious situations could have been prevented, but would have stood in the way of Dwight proving his 007-ness.

His first boat was not a boat, but a canoe, which he purchased in anticipation of the Inferno Flood. This flood was bigger than normal, however, and ran four feet up the side of our condo. It happened so fast and so early that it was impossible to vacate, so the entire neighborhood relocated to their rooftops to wait for it to drain. Most people brought their Weber barbecues with coolers of food, but my mom insisted on hauling up her portable TV because she hadn't missed an episode of Oprah since it entered national syndication in 1986.

The morning of the flood, there were Dwight; his wife, Bethany; and the kids. Bethany was a sliver of a woman, which made it hard to believe her two kids could be so plump. Duke, the eldest, had a mound of red hair that had yet to meet a comb, and looked like he spent the majority of his fifteen years eating bacon. His younger brother, Grady, was quiet like his mother and spent every free moment reading comics. The whole lot of them came paddling toward our condo in a sea of muddy water ricocheting off pieces of neighbors' lawn furniture. And suddenly, as Dwight explains it, "A big rat started coming for the boat."

"Rat! Rat!" he yelled as he pulled out his rifle and started shooting at it. The more he shot, the faster it swam toward him. It should be noted that Dwight had very poor vision, and the rat was, in fact, a wet squirrel.

The 1985 Fourth of July celebration proved to be one of Dwight's more unfortunate 007 moments. He lost partial vision in both his eyes while trying to light a metal bucket of firecrackers with a welding torch. Since James Bond would never be caught dead wearing corrective lenses, neither would Dwight. I imagine, however, if Mr. Bond ever felt the aching desire to ignite a metal bucketful of firecrackers, he might don a pair of welding glasses.

Bang! Bang! Two final shots before Dwight crawled to the back of the canoe, climbing over his life's possessions and family.

Since the "rat" wasn't relenting, he told Bethany and the kids to "jump ship." I like to think that advising family members to jump out of a canoe into dirty river water is a solution only someone who has spent a significant amount of time in the South would have come up with, someone who has never tried to jump from a canoe.

Bethany and the kids jumped head first into a body of water that was only four feet deep. They could have simply stepped in. For the kids it was nothing new; they had always treated the Sheyenne River like their very own swimming pond.

Next thing we knew, the "rat" found its way onto a piece of floating lumber and then leaped into the canoe.

"Motherfucker's in the boat! Motherfucker's in the boat!"

Regardless of a "rat" running amuck in his canoe, Dwight didn't jump out. Oh no, he kept shooting, blowing holes in his own canoe, shooting holes in the only thing he could call home until he moved into the Lucky 7—yet again. The squirrel was much better at dodging bullets than Dwight was at shooting them. It scurried to the front, running between his legs, and Dwight ended up shooting himself in the foot. I think we all saw that coming. It seemed to sting a great deal, and for a while he started hopping in pain around the canoe, but once you start hopping in a canoe, you're not far from no longer hopping in a canoe. To the delight of the spectators covering the neighboring rooftops, Dwight fell backward into the murky water. The squirrel remained on the bow eating from a bag of chili flavored Fritos until the vessel finally sank.

The next year Dwight bought an aluminum boat with a Mercury outboard motor. I can only assume he did this to add a sense of recreation to his yearly "vacation." He bought it from a guy in Detroit Lakes, Minnesota, and hauled it back home by strapping it to the top of his Chevy Nova. Coincidently, that was the year the floodwaters jumped the sandbag barrier and spread itself across Sheyenne Street, almost four feet up the side of the middle school.

That morning all of us who were living in the dry part of town eventually made our way down the connecting streets, right up to the water's edge, to witness our Sheyenne Street flowing like a river. It was overwhelming. People stood in shock, not saying much more than "I can't believe it, I just can't believe it." I remember the feeling of helplessness when occasionally a personal possession could be spotted bobbing in the water: a child's doll or a woman's hat.

Reverend Sonnenberg came by and asked the large group of us to bow our heads while he lead us in a prayer.

"Dear heavenly Father, we ask that you bring comfort to the victims of this horrible ..."

Wwwzzzzzzz! A loud, abrasive whirling sound came from behind us. We all lifted our heads, turned around, and there, surrounded by devastation, was Dwight, racing down Sheyenne Street in his new motorboat, with his oldest son, Duke, being pulled on water skis. Bethany was in the front of the boat with a video camera trying to capture Duke as he maneuvered around people's floating possessions. After spotting us halfway down the block, they waved with pride, as if we were all resorting at Club Med. While accompanied by the song "Dixie" blaring from his musical boat horn, Dwight stood firing pistols into the air. Not a pretty picture, but it didn't stop people from pulling out their cameras to capture a bit of proof for those that might have missed it.

At a position near our group, Duke pulled his back foot out of the slalom ski in preparation for kicking a piece of trash into the air like a football. An orange obstacle that looked similar to a trash bag barely floated above water, after being covered in the wake of the boat. Duke cocked his leg back and at the precise moment unleashed his foot and launched the orange mass into the air. Even thought it flew directly at us, it was hard to identify the object for all the dirty water rapidly windmilling off it. The hunk of trash landed at our feet with a *splat*! It wasn't a piece of litter after all. It was the decapitated body of my Winnie the Pooh bear. His legs spread open wide, revealing my mother's telltale stitching that zigzagged up the crotch. Mom gave me a wry smile that seemed to say: *Yes, I know you fucked the bear.*

The prayer group turned their attention back to the Lord, pretending nothing had happened, in a way only midwesterners can do. But something did happen. As we bowed our heads that afternoon, my religious beliefs were challenged for the very first time. Actually, I'm sure they were challenged many times before—after all I lived in Fargo—but I was never listening. I spent my life dancing the dance of religion but never feeling the true beat. With the soles of my shoes nearly in water, I acknowledged the irony of asking for swift comfort from the very deity who allowed this discomfort to occur in the first place. Not to mention, one who intentionally created a human being who would choose to water-ski in sewer water.

For the previous two years, I allowed doubts about Christianity to linger only in the shadowy parts of my mind, not wanting to rattle my mother's faith. I knew I would be leaving soon enough and could seek answers at that time. Mom is a happy person who loves attending church, and I want her to stay that way. So for the last two years, I've continued to sit quietly next to her in the pew, dancing the dance.

Yet, strangely enough, we bonded at church in a way we never did at home. As with most mothers, everything she did or said bothered me. But every week at St. Andrews Lutheran Church, we were confidants in an exercise to bridge the tediousness of the service. Singing was fun, and reciting prayers and creeds was fine; but following the sermon was dull work, and listening to the weekly amateur hour when a regular parishioner, be it the mailman or the grocer, would stumble through a gospel reading was more than we could stomach.

So when Mom would lean over to me in the middle of yet another boring baptism and in her loud whisper ask, "Should we go to Tower City for breakfast?" all I could do was smile and feel comforted that she was also bored. When I looked over and found her sketching out the design for what was going to become a game of hangman on the church bulletin, I always thought, *I've got the best mom a kid could ask for.*

In retrospect, I was bored by the formality of the Sunday services, but there was a certain spirituality that I couldn't deny or define … but I could point at. It was in the details, where I guess God probably resides. *He* was certainly in the camaraderie my mother built between us after rummaging through her purse for a stick of Wrigley's during the benediction, removing the foil, tearing it in two, and surreptitiously handing me a half, like we were two kids getting away with something. In those moments she filled me with a truly joyful spirit that most parishioners can only pretend to possess in any given service.

After the destruction and insensitivity during the water-skiing demonstration, I thought, *There is no one more in need of "God's details" than Dwight and his family.* I would be the last person to join the Lord's "witnessing" campaign, but out of curiosity, I wondered if a positive energy could be infused into Dwight's family for attending service every Sunday. So I made it my mission to turn Dwight's family toward the bounty of God and away from the various reckless choices of skiing in sewage, using fireworks to melt ice on their driveway, or stealing stop signs from neighboring towns in order to construct an aluminum tool shed. Their time had come, and I was their savior.

Of all the religious denominations, I was convinced that Dwight belonged with the Lutherans; after all, a Lutheran is the lazy man's Catholic. Catholics have a lot of kneeling and getting back up and then kneeling again. Too much work for a Sunday morning. I had no game plan, but in the best interest of our community, I made my way over to the Lucky 7 motel that afternoon to give them my best "Come to Jesus" speech.

Dwight answered the door in a pair of Confederate flag boxers, and Duke had his leg propped up on the bed with a bag of ice on his knee—an injury I can only deduce happened because of the unexpected water weight of Winnie's body.

"Hell's bells, look who it is!" blared Dwight. "What can I do for ya, little man?"

"I come bearing good news, Dwight." ·

"You're havin' a barbecue?"

That it was. I had no idea what I was going to say, until that moment. Dwight handed me the perfect approach. This man loved barbequing more than life itself. I speculate it gave him an excuse to play with fire. Anytime he was invited to someone's house for a backyard BBQ, which wasn't often, he made a beeline across the lawn and nudged his way, like a ram in heat, through the huddle of men around the grill.

"I'm not sure if you know this or not, but St. Andrews Lutheran Church is holding a fundraising barbecue at the end of the month, and I know they're always looking for volunteers to man the grill."

"I can man the grill," he said, lecherously. "Tell 'em, I'll do it." He turned like a gunfighter toward the others in the room and declared, "I'm 'Q'in' in church Sunday! Yee haa!"

"Whoa, whoa, hold on; you can't just show up and expect to take over."

"I can't?"

"No, you need to make a good showing in church a couple times first. You know, let them know you mean business when it comes to the Lord. Understand what I'm saying?"

"Hell, yeah."

"And that you'll have the Lord's best interest at heart when standing at the grill."

"I'm there." Again, he impulsively turned to his family and yelled out, "Git your Sunday-go-to-meetin' gear on, we're headin' to church! Yee haa!"

"No! No! No! Dwight, today's only Thursday."

"Fuck!"

Sunday finally came, and I couldn't have been more motivated to attend a church service in my life. Shamefully, my interest in their family's emotional growth took a backseat to the likelihood that their family would set fire to an old lady's wig. What can I say? My job was done. Dwight and his family circus were front and center so no man could mistake the level of their devotion.

It was an extremely hot morning, and with the floodwaters still lingering, the humidity was palpable. Despite the heat, the ten pews with a split down the middle were packed. Mom and I sat three rows behind and across the aisle to give us the optimum view. Of course, no seat impaired a parishioner from viewing the ten-gallon hat that was perched on Dwight's head. It was an identical match to the one Duke was wearing.

The organ began an uplifting piece of music that set a tone of positivity and high energy. At the height of the chorus, Reverend Sonnenberg opened the side door, and in great ceremony, made his way to the front of the stage. Dwight, like a school kid, immediately raised his hand. It was clear the reverend had noticed both the hand and the hat, but was in no state of mind to deal with whatever it signified. He averted his eyes as he approached the center aisle and took an extremely sharp left turn toward the altar. After bowing his head in a moment of private prayer, which appeared to go on longer than usual, he spread his arms open wide and said, "God bless you one and all; the Lord Jesus Christ is your savior." The crowd responded as usual, "Amen." At this point in the service the reverend would usually turn to the congregation, and in a casual and civilian manner address the crowd. Often he would go so far as to stroll down the center aisle while acknowledging certain members of the congregation who had birthdays, anniversaries, or the like. That particular morning however, he delivered his "welcome" speech with his back to us. He spoke and gestured as if he were standing before us, but in fact, we were behind him.

Let us not forget, Reverend Sonnenberg had not fully recovered from the emotional whiplash of his son becoming a woman. The event had taken the pigment from his hair and the spirit from his eyes. His heart had shrunk, and the very fibers that kept him standing had all but unraveled in a heap at the bottom of his soul. He had no energy left for anything else. So when a man in a ten-gallon hat was raising his hand in the front row, Reverend Sonnenberg had no choice but to ignore it with great defiance. In this instance, he ignored it by pretending his congregation was the back wall.

Dwight was unrelenting and kept his hand held high on the likely chance that the "preacher man" would eventually turn around. The preacher man did not, and this was of no use to Dwight, who was only there to make his presence known so that he might be placed in charge of St. Andrews Lutheran grill. After the first song was sung, during which Dwight's hand remained in the air, his eyes fixed on the reverend, he removed his hat and used it to add additional length to his raised arm. At this point the reverend had no choice but to finally approach the podium and face and address the congregation. Everyone was on pins and needles, wondering how he would confront this disruption. The reverend stepped forward and adjusted the microphone as Dwight visibly inched his arm up even higher by lifting an ass cheek off the surface of the pew. He peered out over the parishioners for several seconds, which felt like minutes, until finally referring back to his Bible and asking us to join in on the reading of the Lord's Prayer.

No one moved a muscle, and Reverend Sonnenberg began on his own, "Our Father, which art in heaven …"

Bam! Like a mousetrap that had engaged, Dwight snapped his hat down on his knee for the entire world to hear and stormed out with his family trailing behind. A few people picked up with the reverend in reciting the text, and by the time Dwight was out the front door everyone had joined in and things went on like nothing had happened.

But for Dwight something had happened, He missed out on flipping burgers for the Lord.

More often than not, if you are born in North Dakota, you will be required to go to church and attend Sunday school until the day of your confirmation. Sunday after eternal Sunday you sit there in tight, bunched-up clothes, kicking the chair in front of you while pretending to listen. Because you are there against your will, like a prisoner, you don't care enough to challenge the philosophies you're presented, biding your days, until the end is all you care about. Then one day you're an adult and find yourself huddled in a prayer group with flood waters splashing at your heels, and it makes you wonder: Who's in charge here? They say ignorance is bliss, and "they" have never said a more true statement. For the most part, people in Fargo don't challenge religion. They have nothing to gain by challenging it, and everything to loose. If there's a heaven, they're going, if not, it's no skin off their back to show up every Sunday in church and sing some songs.

My mother believes that God has a plan for everyone. God certainly has a great plan for the people of Fargo … and the plan reveals itself every spring in the form of a flood.

FOURTH STREET
Tupperware Party

As I roll to a stop at Fourth Street, I look over at my life's possessions stacked from floor mat to dome light, impeding the use of my passenger side mirror. The feeling of melancholy that I felt a few streets back has exploded and sent waves of sadness throughout my body. The idea of life on my own has just hit me and is completely sobering. I'm slowly realizing that once you leave home, you can never go back. It can never be the same. Exactly what imperceptible part of my soul or personality will I lose upon leaving? That scares the hell out of me in this moment.

I move a big Tupperware container full of Chex Mix so I can see more clearly down Fourth Street. It's deserted, and I'm considering turning back. Fourth Street for five blocks, right on Elm, and a left on Circle Drive would have me back home in less than four minutes. Simple. Easy. My mom would invite me back with open arms, and we'd go about the rest of our day as if nothing had happened.

I snap open the top of the container and take in the nurturing smell of warm Chex Mix. I'm sure Mom sent it along for that very reason: to remind me of home. The container is still warm. I feel as if I squeezed just a little harder, my fingers would mold themselves into the white plastic. Mom branded our last name on all her Tupperware with a black marker to ensure their safe return after a church function or leaving some leftover casserole behind for the neighbors. This particular piece has been washed so many times for so many years that the name is nothing but a faint impression.

Mom loved Tupperware like one of her own kids. She took it everywhere. We'd often run late for events because she would say, "Oh, let's just throw some snacks into a Tupperware and take it along," and proceeded to spend the next twenty minutes searching for the right lid. She had more lids than containers, but none of the lids fit any of the containers. Very often I would be at a friend's house and see a Tupperware container with our name on it. No lid of course, just the bowl. Our Tupperware got around. It was trampy. I never had a lunch box in elementary school; Mom just threw a sandwich and chips into a lemonade pitcher.

Tupperware went everywhere we went, including the Crown Movie Theater, which used to sit on the corner of Fourth Street, but has since burned down. There are a lot of decent, upstanding people who attend the movies, and then there are those who go to the movies to eat—like my mother. The only thing worse than her eating is that she brings her own food. Five minutes into the movie, Tupperware containers full of M&M's, Whoppers, and lemon drops are yanked out of her purse like a set of maracas. And shaking them at us was her way of asking if we wanted some. Once the sweets were distributed, out came the grocery sack full of popcorn—enough for everyone in the theater. And believe me, by the time she yanked it out of her bag, everyone in the theater knew it was there. If that weren't enough to drive them from their seats, her rolling down the sides of the bag to make it more accessible would be. Apparently, she was the only one who didn't realize just how loud a brown paper sack is.

"Mom, please!"

"Oh, they're not paying any attention to me; they're watchin' the movie."

"They can't hear the movie."

Then, just when people settled from throwing us glaring looks, she'd rifle through her purse again, all the way to the bottom this time, down to where the Shasta pop settled. Fifteen cents a can at your local supermarket or a buck twenty-five per case. It comes in grape, orange, lemon-lime, root beer, and many other flavors to tantalize the teenage tongue. But does Mom get us one of those? No. She gets us cream soda. Why? Does she think we like it? No, she thinks we *should* like it.

"Oh, don't get your undies in a bunch; it's an acquired taste."

During the years I was attending college, every third Saturday morning I awoke to the cackling sounds of a Tupperware party that my mother would host. The only bathroom in our condominium was downstairs, and my bedroom was upstairs. Often I sat at the top of the stairs with a full bladder, considering whether to suffer the misery of passing through a group of women, or just peeing in my garbage can.

"… Then after I had just made a potato chip casserole, like the one we're eating now, Scott walked in and announced he was eating at a friend's house, dontchaknow. 'Why didn't you tell me? I just made a perfectly good potato chip casserole.' And he said, 'Well, why didn't you tell me you were making a casserole?' Kids. And then he begrudgingly offered to cancel his plans and I said, 'No, it's just a potato chip casserole. Nothing important, it'll freeze. That's what Tupperware is for,'" I heard my mom babbling from the belly of the party.

All the women laughed while shoving their faces with forkfuls of potato chip casserole. That's why midwesterners tend to be overweight; they like to crush potato chips onto their dinners, which results in casserole-ass—or, as my dad liked to call it, "asserole."

From the top of the stairs I knew better than to think passing through meant just passing through. *Passing through* meant they would inquire about my past week and then deconstruct it until every interesting piece of gossip was revealed. My only game plan was to begin making some noise so the excitement of my actually appearing on the stairs wouldn't provoke such animated reaction. With God on my side, I might actually be able to slip past without having to talk to anyone.

"Scott must be up. He's been tired since his trip to the Vikings game."

"I would be so nervous with my son visiting a big city like Minneapolis," Sharon said.

Mom reminded her I was twenty-three, old enough for a trip.

"He had lunch with Oprah," Frances said, having confused "eating in the same restaurant" and "eating with."

"Really? What was she eating?" some foreign voice chimed in as I landed on the bottom step.

"Oh, here he is; good morning, dear. Say hi to the Tupperware girls."

"Hi, Tupperware girls. I'm going to the—"

"Honey, tell them about meeting Oprah," mom said, stopping me in my tracks before I could escape to the bathroom.

They all slipped quickly into the deluded belief that I had made some actual contact with Oprah.

"Yes, your mother was telling us you had lunch with her; how exciting."

"I really wasn't—"

Ester interrupted, "What was she eating?"

"I don't know."

"Something fatty?"

"Again, I don't—"

"Salad?"

"Poor woman just can't keep her weight down," Marge said as a flake of potato chip fell from her lip.

"Does she have acrylics?"

"What?"

"Or real? I bet they're real," Frances said, turning to Sharon, who nodded in agreement as I made another step in the direction of the bathroom.

"Scott, don't use the toilet. Carl's coming over later to fix it," Mom said while holding out a Tupperware pitcher. "If you can't hold it, sweetie, go in this."

"*What?*" Marge said, repulsed.

"He had bladder trouble. I don't want to aggravate it and have him start wetting the bed again."

"Mom!"

"Besides, it'll clean up nicely."

"I heard you can put Tupperware in the dishwasher now; is that so?" Sharon asked Marge.

"Absolutely."

Frances, my favorite of Mom's friends because she's an instigator, said, "I wouldn't."

"It says right on the bottom, 'Dishwasher safe,'" Marge declared, holding up a bowl.

"Mine's all bent out of shape. It doesn't burp anymore."

"Then it's not Tupperware."

"It's Tupperware."

"Well, I'm sorry, but it's not."

"Tupperware!"

"I've been in Tupperware for twenty years. If anyone knows Tupperware, it's Marge Anderson, and when Tupperware says it's dishwasher safe, goddamn it, it's dishwasher safe!"

The room went silent. In Fargo the phrase "goddamn it" is used only when someone really means business.

"That reminds me," Sharon asked, dodging the unpleasantness in the room, "did that bedwetting machine work well? My Patrick is still having trouble wetting at night."

"Like a charm," my mom said, "once I discovered to put the wiring under the sheets. You would think it woulda come with directions. Unfortunately, Scott got a few nasty shocks before we figured that out. But he stopped wetting eventually, so there you go."

"Do you still have it?"

"Sure, would you like to use it? Scott, run out to the garage. It's in a box marked *Kids' Toys*."

"Mom, I don't think that's such a good idea."

"Sure it is."

"Fine. Let me go to the bathroom first?" I made my way into the bathroom to pee into what may have been my grade school lunch box.

Ding! Ding!

I look up to find Denise Sonnenberg's blue bicycle as it pulls around my idle vehicle. "Scott, you're leaving this morning?"

"Right now, in fact," I tell her.

"Well, good luck out there. I know you'll be great."

"Thanks, Denise."

"Will you come back?" she asks delicately.

"I don't know. Depends on what I find out there."

"Afraid?"

"I wasn't yesterday. But as I'm about to hit the highway … yeah, a little, I guess."

She gives an understanding nod and says, "Well, you won't be content until you do find out what's out there. Trust me, you will never regret making the trip."

That feels comforting to me. If I regret the move, I can always come back. And in that thought, I realize the choice Denise made was one that could not be reversed. I could turn my car around in Los Angeles and return home, but once you surgically remove your penis, it will never grow back. Again the leaving gives me the boldness to ask, "Do you … have you ever felt regret?"

The forwardness of the question forces Denise to shift her gaze to the fruit and flowers in the wicker basket strapped to the handlebars.

"I regret not doing it sooner." She smiles, frees a single daisy from the bouquet, and hands it through my window. "Drive safely. Good-bye." And with that she peddles off, punctuating the departure with another clank of her silver bell.

Ding! Ding!

I know I will miss home, because the farther away I get from it this morning, the more powerful it becomes. God, it was nothing more than four walls just fifteen minutes ago. Think of that. Its power will be overwhelming by the time I reach the West Coast. And so, too, I imagine, will be the scent of Chex Mix in this well-worn container. And, I *will* "get home again," if for no other reason than to return this piece of Tupperware to its rightful owner.

THIRD STREET
Bingo Charlie

As I drive past Smokey's Steak House on Third Street, I can almost hear the echoes of former "bingos" resonating in my head. Every Friday, Smokey's hosted an evening of bingo, sponsored by the American Legion for the junior high hockey association. For the last five years, "Bingo!" has been the call of the wild that rocks through the Midwest every night of the week. It replaced the old call of the wild, which was "Go fish!" Midwesterners have finally found an activity to fill the void between bowling nights. Only in the Midwest could a game like bingo, usually reserved for nursing homes, catch on and spread like wildfire.

Of course, the "call" has reached Fargo as well, but there it's not so much a call as it is an apology. The modest people of Fargo feel guilty when they bingo because it means they took the chance away from someone else. So yelling it out becomes painful. In any other state people yell with pride, "Bingo!" The louder and quicker the better: "Bingo!" Rightfully, it should start in the toes, and by the time it gets to the mouth it becomes a shout to the Gods. Tears of joy would not be unreasonable. And multiple bingos are okay as well, because you want to make sure the caller has heard you and stops drawing numbers. The scream should have a Southern Baptist enthusiasm to it.

But in Fargo it's: "Excuse me, I've got a ... I'm sorry."

And Carl the announcer would call out the next number, "B-8! B-8!"

"Oh no. No, no. I've got, um ... Bing ... It's a diagonal. I don't mean to ... Hello? I just wanted to let you know, I've got a ..."

"G-32! G-32!"

"Carl? Excuse me, Carl. Yoo-hoo, Carl ... Bing ... If it's okay with everyone else, that is, I would like to announce that I've managed to ... uhh, three numbers ago I got a diagonal thingy."

Sometimes in life you're given a prophetic sign promising to change the entire scope of your life, rendering you eternally grateful. Roy, the fortune-teller outside the Stop & Shop, never gave me one of those signs, but bingo did.

During my senior year in college I started growing depressed about what to do with my life. I went to college under the guise of using the time to figure out my goals, but in reality I knew what I wanted—I was simply afraid to pursue it. But it was my final year and the clock was ticking. A choice to move to LA had to be followed through on or forgotten entirely. I had also spent my entire life selfishly living off my mother, and the guilt of allowing her to support the family alone was finally emerging. Witnessing the maternal wear and tear of raising two kids should have been enough to inspire me to at least alleviate some of the financial burden ... but it did not. I continued along in a life-coma and needed a jolt of some kind. I needed the universe to slap me in the face. And it did, one Friday night at bingo.

Many of my dateless Friday nights I spent playing bingo with Mom. I gave up on church once I graduated from high school, so Mom and I sort of lost our place to bond, until one night when I begrudgingly joined her for bingo. It quickly became this magical place where I talked to her about things I might never talk to her about across our kitchen table. We would laugh and enjoy ourselves as if we'd forgotten we were related.

At six thirty we picked up Frances the hairdresser and headed over for the big Friday night jackpot. The excitement starts at eight, but we usually arrive at seven in order to get the lucky table. It's not so much the *lucky* table as it is the *only* table. If you're not crafty enough to get the lucky table, you spend the entire night negotiating your bingo cards on the piece of plywood that is precariously placed over the pool table. Or you're at one of the many tree trunks that serve as tables because the owners thought it would be clever to have people eat their meals off logs. It was clever for a moment, but now those five minutes are over and you get the feeling people would rather throw their table into the fire and eat off their laps.

My mother's archenemy Nita also felt she and her best friend Marge the Tupperware queen should have complete ownership over the lucky table and would create a scene if she walked in and found us sitting in "her" spot. There was a day when they were all friends and could sit together in love and joy at the same bingo table, but that day is no longer. Mom and Frances can tolerate Marge, but rumor has it, Nita was unhappy that my mother told Frances that Nita had gone to Minneapolis to get her teeth capped. But it had nothing to do with my mother's motor mouth. Nita had smoked most of her life and was known by everyone to have the most revolting set of teeth in the county. So given the meddling nature of Fargonians, why she figured she could just show up one day with a white picket fence nestled into her gums and not have anyone take note, is beyond me. The dentist's workmanship was so shoddy she could have crawled naked out of a spaceship, and the only thing people would have noticed was the three-ring circus of porcelain in her mouth. Nita's anger at the dentist needed to be misdirected at someone, and that someone was my mom. After that, the war was on, and the three of us had to show up an hour early for bingo, forcing Marge and Nita to straddle a log.

At Smokey's Steakhouse there are players who regard bingo as something other than just bingo. They play as if Howard Cosell were calling the numbers. But it's not Howard at all; it's merely Carl Phillips from the hardware store. It's just Carl, and it's just bingo. In bingo there is no Super Bowl, no World Series, and no Stanley Cup. There is simply a jackpot at the end of the night. There will be no awards ceremony, and they will not play the national anthem before awarding the cash prize. Gatorade will not be poured surprisingly over the victor's head, and you will not be ceremoniously paraded around the room on the shoulders of two American Legion members. Even if you were to be paraded around, good luck finding a Legion member not riddled with osteoporosis. Not only will you not be celebrated, you will be secretly hated. While shaking your hand and patting you lovingly on the back, they will hate you for stealing what was to be their money.

The equipment used in bingo is very simple. Before each game you buy as many game sheets as you can keep track of, and every time a number is called you mark it using a *dauber*, which is essentially a fifty-cent bottle of colored water with a two-cent sponge attached to the top. If you don't have a dauber, Smokey's will sell you one for five dollars. If you're thrifty, you'll buy daubers in bulk, like my mother, and keep five or six of them in your purse at all times so as not to get screwed by Smokey's. During one of Mom's many art classes at the community center, she fashioned a key chain out of an old dauber, so now any time I'm forced to rely on Mom to drive me to a scheduled event, I allow an extra fifteen minutes for her to wade through her purse in search of the one dauber that will start her car.

Assuming you've brought your own dauber, bingo is so simple and cheap to play that it usually attracts the stingiest of village idiots. The level of player eccentricity defies any believability unless witnessed by your very own eyes. One of the more colorful nitwits is the local prostitute, who's known countywide as Stinky. Aside from being intellectually unstable, Stinky is superstitious. Every night she has a dozen miniature trolls lined up in front of her bingo cards. For every missed bingo, she grabs a troll and begins spanking it on the butt, accompanied by a verbal scolding: "Bad troll! Bad, bad troll! Mommy puts you in time-out when you don't win for her." She then lays the troll flat down on her log, which I can only assume proves to be a lesson for the rest of them. "You're flat on your back now, aren't you? If you don't start helping Mommy win, Mommy's going to eat your head."

One night Frances noticed that during the past couple of weeks Stinky had been playing with more bingo sheets than she would normally try to spread out on her log. Frances probably noticed because Stinky started winning two or three jackpots per night.

Finally, one Friday night after she bingoed for the $500 blackout, a Legion member who was verifying the win shouted out, "Not a good bingo!" The place fell silent, and the game continued in a haze of distraction. It was later reported that Stinky, to save money, had been taking her old bingo sheets home and washing the dauber ink off. She was found out because the serial numbers didn't correlate with the sheets that were being sold that night. Stinky's bingo privileges were suspended for a month. The people of Fargo may have their faults, but they are a forgiving lot.

Insanity was not confined to Stinky's table however, for Frances and my mother had purchased a doll named Bingo Charlie who claimed to bring the owner luck. Charlie was a tiny little man made out of pipe cleaners, with jiggly eyes and a fanciful top hat that screamed, "Look at me! I'm a gay pipe cleaner." He was purchased at a rummage sale in a Ziploc bag, and as I always say, there is nothing as effective as second hand luck. I don't know what was more shocking, the fact that someone had the unmitigated audacity to charge twenty-five cents for this "Special Ed" craft project, or the fact that I was an offspring of the woman who purchased it.

"Mom," I pleaded, "nothing says 'I'm useless' like a lucky charm pipe cleaner in the discount bin at a rummage sale. Did you ever think it was there because it didn't work?"

"Oh, gosh no. I figure someone probably had their fill of winning and just wanted to spread it around."

That was some truly imaginative thinking on her part. I myself had trouble believing the previous owners had bingoed their way into retirement and thought it was only right to let some other bingo buddy in on the winning.

"Besides," she argued, "it came with a poem."

How that was an argument in her favor I will never know. To me it was all the more reason *not* to buy it. To Frances it was worthy of her epitaph, and she recited the poem at any inappropriate opportunity. You should understand, of course, in my eyes any opportunity was inappropriate. Not only would she recite this embarrassment of literature, but she would also make Charlie accompany her by dancing him around in circles on the rim of what usually proved to be her fifth vodka tonic.

My name is Bingo Charlie;
I'm here to bring you luck.
Play with me in front of you;
I'll help you win a buck.

After such a display I couldn't help but wonder how those two could justify making fun of Stinky.

Surprisingly enough, while Charlie was in good health, he brought them well over twenty-five cents worth of good luck. But tragically, during one of Frances's nightly poetry readings, Charlie lost his footing and slipped deep into the potent waters of her vodka tonic. By the time he finally surfaced, his jiggly eyes had fallen off, his hat had lost most of its flare, and the overabundance of luck that he possessed was washed away. Charlie had danced for the last time and was put to rest with the trolls.

It has always been my experience that the older women are, the more possessive they become with their winnings. On the rare occasion that there are simultaneous winners, it is understood that the earnings will be split. And until the incident with Agnes and Myrtle, it was an unwritten rule. Now, however, it is handwritten on a very large sheet of paper that is posted at the front door. This is only until they can afford to display the information in neon. Agnes and Myrtle are women so elderly they require other people to mark the numbers for them on their cards. Otherwise, by the time they find the number called and muster up enough energy to push down on the dauber, they're three numbers behind. Their involvement in their own game is so minimal that they could call in on a speakerphone from the hospital bed—where they rightly belonged—and no one would be the wiser—least of all, them.

This made it all the more amazing the day Myrtle and Agnes simultaneously bingoed on a two-hundred-dollar jackpot and, in a selfish rage, turned it into a brawl. Myrtle, in a hysterical fit of anger, crawled and fell over her log and began choking Agnes from behind. Startled by the attack, and surprised like the rest of us that

Myrtle's legs could support her own weight, Agnes fell out of her chair and onto the floor. Locked in a bear hug, the women started to tumble on the floor like the Geriatric Championship Belt was at stake. The floor was beginning to collect daubers, drinks, and toppled log tables. Meanwhile, Carl, who is more than slightly deaf, hadn't heard the women yell "bingo," and he was continuing to call numbers. Stinky, who wouldn't stop playing for her own funeral, was still marking the numbers despite the fact that most of her troll collection had been knocked off her log.

By this point, Agnes had maneuvered her way to Myrtle's head and given a yank on her hair, which wasn't really her hair, but a wig that looked as if it had been purchased in the same discount bin as Bingo Charlie. Myrtle was left with nothing but an old nylon stocking that she had used to hide her original hair, which happened to be a strange shade of blue-gray. Startled by the mass of hair in her hand, Agnes screamed and threw it high into the air. As the wig flew end over end into the rafters, life seemed to shift into slow motion. I looked around and wondered: *What the hell is going on?*

My mother and I shared experiences, but never the *joy* of an experience until that night. In this strange suspension of time, I could see that I was having as much fun watching old women wrestle on the floor as she was. I saw her for the first time as a woman, not a mother. Who is this person I call Mom sitting next to me? All I know about her is what serves my life. She makes me grilled cheese sandwiches with bologna inside. She buys me things whether she wants to or not. She washes my clothes. She loves me whether she wants to or not.

Through the laughter I saw her worn face and tired eyes and thought: *I did that to her.* She was once a homecoming queen, and now she is just an exhausted mother. I had always been too involved with my own life to recognize that she had at one time lived for herself and not for me. I remembered seeing the picture Helen showed me of my mom in high school, when she was young, beautiful, and full of potential. She looked to be someone who had grand dreams; dreams that could break free of the insidious pull of Fargo. She appeared to be someone who would be unaffected by the magnetism of smallness and safety, someone who might attend polo events and poke fun at bingo players. She would sip mint juleps on her yacht while telling the grandchildren stories of her childhood escape from the small, backward town of Fargo to the opulent life of Cape Cod.

But she did none of that. Instead, she spent her life sacrificing for my brother and me. And while I'm thankful she did it, and I do love her for it, I have realized I don't want to be a fifty-year-old bingo player. In thirty years, when someone looks at an old photo of me, I don't want him to feel compelled to say, "He had so much potential." This was the slap in the face my complacent life needed. Right then and there, in the chaos of the bingo brawl, I realized I had to take the chance my mother never did. I had to risk; and in order to risk, I had to leave Fargo.

Sadly, last summer Smokey's Steakhouse announced they would no longer be hosting nightly bingo. It was the same old story: small time, mom-and-pop bingo forced out by big-time corporate bingo. Sure, bingo was still offered in the basement of the Catholic Church every Saturday, but they served only boxed Mogen David wine, which was no competition for the fully stocked bar that the corporate bingo parlor offered. Eventually, the overwhelming desire to play bingo and drink hard liquor brought the masses to their knees, and corporate bingo welcomed them with open arms and a happy hour.

The new attraction was located on the outskirts of town and was surrounded by a large, presumptuous parking lot. It was named Big Top Bingo and had all the cliché design trappings of a circus. It was a large, red-and-white striped tent framed by two large floodlights that swirled around in the sky like a Hollywood movie premier. Inside there were jugglers, stilt walkers, and clowns shaping balloons into animals—everything you would ever want in a circus, but nothing you wanted in a bingo parlor. Nita and her teeth fit in perfectly. But what it really had going for it was there were more than enough tables for everyone, and not one of the tables was a log.

Two weeks before I was going to leave town, Mom, Frances, and I all tried to rekindle our love for the game under the big top, but it just wasn't the same. We left early that night and never looked back. As exciting as it was to have the caller spit fire from his mouth between numbers, I couldn't help but miss Carl and his inarticulate drivel. I realize memory is a liar, but now when I think back on it, I can honestly hear a little Howard Cosell in Carl's voice as it echoes in my mind.

SECOND STREET
Sour Cream Raisin Pie

I imagine when most people drive past the old, rusted-out Scoop Shack sign they see failure. But as I sit here at the stop sign measuring my fate, questioning whether I have the strength to accelerate forward another block without turning back, I gather courage from Hilbert and Ester's efforts. They tried for years to have kids, but no luck, so they decided to do the next best thing. They opened an ice-cream shop: the Scoop Shack. Hilbert sold his farmland outside of Mapleton, which had been farmed by a local neighbor since Hilbert had no skills or knowledge of farming. When he was a child, his father, who owned the land and eventually passed it along to him, was so protective of his only son that he didn't want to risk him being injured by any farm implements, and therefore never allowed him to work the fields. So young Hilbert spent all his days with his mother developing kitchen skills.

Little Hilbert's favorite kitchen activity was making homemade ice cream. Since he didn't have any siblings to play with, he occupied his time perfecting the many different flavors he invented. His mother also taught him how to prepare waffle batter and bake his own cones. This remained strictly a hobby throughout most of his early adulthood as he made a living working as a short-order cook for the truck stop diner in Tower City. It was there that he became famous for a sour cream raisin pie that is still on the menu to this day. My family would often drive the ten miles out of town after Sunday church service just to have a slice. In fact, I plan on pulling over for a piece as I drive through Tower City.

Ester was born and raised in Rollag, Minnesota, the home of the Western Minnesota Steam Threshers Reunion. Every year during Labor Day weekend the local farmers fire up the old Garr engines to thresh with steam for old time's sake, and to bring the past to life for the enjoyment of young and old. Once you've experienced it, it's an event you will never forget, nor attend ever again. To get to Rollag, which has two churches, a craft store, and no bars, you take Interstate 94 to the Downer exit, go through the town of Downer—which incidentally lives up to its name—and once you pass the ditches filled with random tombstones you will be there. I can only assume the tombstones along the way are former spectators who killed themselves out of boredom.

Ester went to a prairie schoolhouse with twelve other students who ranged in age from seven to seventeen. She led the same life that thousands of young women raised on small Midwestern farms lead. They work with their mothers in the kitchen learning all the skills necessary to raise a large family. By the time she was fifteen she could single-handedly prepare brunch, lunch, and dinner for ten farmers during harvest season. After her father injured his back and decided to retire in Florida, Ester moved to Tower City to work in the truck stop that her uncle owned.

She was a waitress at the diner when she met Hilbert, and they were married two years later. Following the death of Hilbert's father, they retired early on the money and bought a big three-bedroom home in Fargo with the idea of starting a large family. The family didn't come. Years later the rooms remained empty. Ester was denied the one thing she had spent her entire childhood preparing to do ... raise a family.

Hilbert felt like he had lost a wife. Once he completed the morning coffee and Word Jumble in the paper, the day was empty. They used to laugh together, cook, and take little day trips to the park for a picnic or a simple walk through the gardens. But at that time, Ester had no energy to vacation, and no interest in even leaving the house. To occupy his free time and attempt to rekindle some joy in his life, Hilbert started back to his childhood hobby of making ice cream. Every Saturday he would set up shop in his garage and give away cones to all of us neighborhood kids. He even transferred his talent for sour cream raisin pie into a flavor of ice cream, which became a favorite among the very elderly … and me. My brother, Todd, and I would often hang out in the garage longer than most kids. We liked his stories from the diner, and more times than not he would spoon us up another scoop or two.

It was in the garage one day that I heard Hilbert telling my mother about Ester's noted absence: "The day Ester found out she was unable to have kids, she shut down; didn't eat much and sort of just stuck to herself in the bedroom, knitting and whatnot. Felt like she let me down as she knew how much I love kids and always wanted many of my own since I never had any kin."

A couple of weeks later, while I was sitting on an old paint can enjoying my cone, I saw Ester peaking through a crack in the open door that led to the garage. The weak, feeble spirit which had been rolling over the hills and valleys of her soul like a fog seemed to lift a little bit when she saw Hilbert's smiling face as the kids laughed and circled his pails of ice cream. His happiness brought a smile to her face, and the next week she joined him in the garage.

Later that summer the bakery at the corner of Second Street and Sheyenne closed its doors, which spurred an idea in Hilbert's head to move his ice-cream business out of his garage and into the old bakery. I believe he hoped in some secret compartment in his heart that this might replace the child they would never have, and sustain Ester's recently recovered joy so that they could get back to being the happy couple they once were.

By the next spring, remodeling had finished, and the Scoop Shack officially opened its doors. It was a pure and simple ice-cream shop, nothing fancy. They didn't have thirty-one flavors. They had four. There was no indoor seating, just a walk-up window with a few stray picnic tables along the outside. The Scoop Shack was open only five months out of the year because North Dakotans are slaves to all four of the seasons, and the seasons don't mess around in Fargo; they demand their equal time. On September 30 it's 110 degrees in the shade and on October 1, fall steps up and says to summer, "Get the hell out of my way," and the next thing you know, it's 40 degrees.

The Scoop Shack was a hit from the very beginning, and lines ran from Second Street all the way to Third. People from surrounding towns would come to cool off after a long day in the field or toiling over a hot stove. Hilbert continued the tradition he started in his garage of giving away free cones to kids on Saturdays. Both Ester and Hilbert loved the children, and we loved Ester and Hilbert. It was exciting to see them out from behind the walk-up window, whether it was at church or the grocery store, and Hilbert always had some kind of treat for you in his pocket; a coin, piece of candy, or a token for a free cone. For those five months out of each year, Ester and Hilbert had the children they always wanted. They became parents every single time a child stepped up to the window.

Going to the Scoop Shack was an event. It took longer than a standard ice-cream shop because Hilbert would bake the cones as he went along, and often the demand would surpass the supply. He hand-rolled the cones, and as they came out of the oven they looked more like deformed burritos, but tasted divine. The hard ice cream would soften perfectly once wrapped snugly in its warm waffle blanket. This was ice cream as an art form—not to be rushed.

The Scoop Shack saved Hilbert and Ester's marriage and patched the hole in their hearts that was punctured by their inability to have kids. They took long vacations in the winter and always brought gifts back for some of their favorites, of which I was one. Ever since I tripped over the sprinkler head in their lawn, I was given preferential treatment. Every year, before they took off for their trip, my mom and I would swing by their house and pick up four gallons of sour cream raisin that Hilbert would make special for me. It was like retrieving a summer day when we'd open the freezer in the dead of winter and spoon up a dish of the Scoop Shack.

And then it happened, and it happened overnight, like an ugly snowstorm that drops four feet of hell on your life and your car. But this was worse ... this was the Dairy Queen. First it was corporate bingo and then corporate ice cream. Five years after the Scoop Shack opened its doors, the DQ rode into town like a cocky, ruthless franchise, cracking its masochistic whip across our collective backs until it was bloody, swollen, and begged for the cool relief that could only be brought on by a Dilly Bar. The only available real estate for the franchise to take root was in the undeveloped part of town, but that didn't matter; it was the DQ after all, and it feared nothing, not even poor location. Come spring, the huge DQ sign arrogantly rested on its lofty pole and flickered its red neon like a big "Fuck You" to the Scoop Shack.

After the corporate dust settled, it was clear that the Scoop Shack was going to be damaged by this. The question was how much? The first attack came after the first year, and it cut deep. Much to our surprise, Molly, a long time assistant at the Scoop Shack, was lured over to the big leagues by an increase in salary and stock options. Hilbert could compete with employee discounts but not stock options, so he gave Molly his blessing and promised to come visit her. And he did.

For some reason he invited Todd and me to join him, maybe as backup if things went wrong. This is what I thought, anyway. But the fact is pretty conclusive that no one would ever need backup in a Dairy Queen. Hilbert told us he viewed the trip to see Molly as an opportunity to pay their competition a visit.

When their olive green Chevy Impala pulled up to the Dairy Queen, neither Ester nor Hilbert budged for what seemed like five minutes. The sound of the engine clicking as it cooled was the only noise. Todd and I just sat there trying to look at each other without moving our heads. There was a heavy energy in the car radiating from the front seat, and the energy vibrating in the backseat was excitement because we had yet to have a fancy desert from the DQ.

Finally Hilbert said, "Well …" and with that, Ester opened her door. The word *Well* in Fargo is often a complete sentence. It's used to initiate a predetermined activity. For example, in a café, after the tip has been placed upon the table, a person might say, "Well," at which point everyone at the table knows it's time to stand and leave. It's also used at the beginning of a sentence for absolutely no reason whatsoever. You can't simply declare, "I think it's a good idea." No, they feel the need to say, "Well, I think it's a good idea." *Well* is the equivalent of *Umm*. Many midwesterners want desperately to be the next person to speak in a given conversation but don't necessarily have anything to say. A perfectly timed *Well* will reserve your place in line and buy you time to formulate a thought before anyone else can jump in.

That crisp morning, *Well* launched us out of the car and up the sidewalk to one of the two glass doors and into the lobby. The noise of the machines made us all dizzy, and the line of people apparently made Hilbert sick to his stomach because he immediately had to sit down on the red padded stools. It appeared as though they wanted to leave, but there was Molly, behind the counter, and so proud to be able to help them. And they too were proud. Their little girl was all grown up and working in the "real" ice-cream racket.

After the line cleared, Molly chimed, "What would you guys like? It's on the house."

"Well," Hilbert started, "it all looks pretty good." Which was a lie, because moments earlier he mumbled something about "too much crap on the menu." Column after column of options, yet none of it made any sense to him; in fact, each option could have used further explanation beyond its title. "Maybe we'll just have a chocolate cone; is that okay with you guys?"

What? Was he crazy? Only a stupid chocolate cone? My blood had drained from my brother's face and I was starting to sweat.

"Yes, that will be fine," Ester agreed.

"Just a cone?" Molly asked. "You sure you don't want a Blizzard or a Parfait or something?"

As far as Hilbert was concerned, she was speaking a different language, words that he was convinced would have translated into dishes that were too complex for his palate, but to be polite he reconsidered the menu board and after a fair amount of time, he concluded, "No, we'll keep it simple, but thank you for offering."

As Molly switched on the fancy contraption that automatically blended the ingredients and pushed it out into a cone, Hilbert folded his hands together into a ball of fingers and let them rest upon his stomach while his head bowed slightly, politely waiting. He looked troubled, and Ester sighed in a manner that suggested she was worried about him. He was not in the ice-cream profession to be the best or to make financial gains. No, he opened the shop simply for Ester, simply to ease the pain and emptiness that she felt over not being able to provide him children. Hilbert had never talked to her about that dark period, but assumed that it still remained with her, and that the joy of the children who came to the Scoop Shack was the only thing that suppressed her overwhelming sadness. I suspect he wanted, on many occasions, to tell her that he loved her just the same, that even though it was his passion to be a father, what truly mattered was their life together. But to his shame, he never did. And while the shiny Dairy Queen machine twirled out the final chocolate cone, Hilbert's eyes watered. He was probably predicting this would bring an eventual end to the Scoop Shack and to the joy in Ester's spirit. Todd and I watched as Ester placed her hand upon the small of his back and gave it a gentle pat. After thirty-five years of marriage she knew exactly how to present a comforting little gesture that spoke to his heart. The tender touch of her warm hand and its nearly undetectable circular pattern never failed to bring a smile to his face.

We ate our chocolate cones in the olive green Chevy Impala accompanied by the sounds of the *Farmers Market* radio show. At the conclusion of the feeder cattle report there was nothing left but the napkins; yet Ester nodded in agreement when Hilbert concluded there was a certain artificiality to the ice cream.

In a desperate attempt to resuscitate his customer base, Hilbert created a monthly "Dollar Days Special" and contracted a company out of Minneapolis to have a six-foot ice-cream-cone balloon constructed to help advertise. The first Sunday of the month, cones were only a dollar, and people came out of the woodwork for them, which brought new life to Ester and Hilbert's faces. Hilbert couldn't contain himself, and kept running out to the line to shake people's hands, pat the little ones' heads, and run right back in. The enthusiasm generated by Sunday Dollar Days lasted only the length of the day. Some of the regulars stuck by the Scoop Shack, but there were no more lines throughout the week. Profit was something Hilbert learned to live without in the hopes of keeping Ester's spirit alive, but the yearly loss was becoming harder and harder to justify.

The Dairy Queen eventually drove Ester and Hilbert out of business. They continued to live in the house directly across from their old business until last year, when Hilbert passed away after contracting pneumonia during a hospital stay. Within the year, Ester moved to Florida with her sister, where she no longer has to deal with scraping frost off a windshield, putting on snow tires, or facing the rusty, old Scoop Shack sign, which still dangles from its post.

Watching the sign wave in the breeze I don't see failure. The Scoop Shack was a beautifully realized dream. Nothing can take away the fact that they woke up one morning, pulled on their boots, and said, "Let's build this together." They didn't stall, sitting in their car at a crossroads, riddled with doubt; they simply pressed the gas pedal and moved forward, never looking back.

FIRST STREET
Miles of Wheat

There's First Street, and my stomach just turned on itself. One more block and I'll be gone. I simply took a straight road to cross eleven intersections in the span of maybe twenty minutes, and yet my heart is in a different place. I shouldn't have driven down Sheyenne Street. Had I known so many memories were going to jar loose, I could have easily taken the gravel road out past the softball diamonds and the fair grounds and been gone by now.

I pull over to the curb and stop in front of Larson's 24-Hour Supermarket, open 8:00 a,m, to 10:00 p.m. It's very quiet at this end of town; there's no foot traffic down here.

It's strange to think that less than an hour ago I opened my eyes to the skyline-like wallpaper of my childhood bedroom. Lying on my bed and staring at the ceiling, I realized it was the last time I'll be waking through these eyes to that ceiling. Next time I'll be a guest, and my eyes will have a deeper focus and a gaze of worldliness. Actually, when I come back to visit, I'll probably be downstairs on the couch. More than likely my bed will have made room for a sewing machine and the closet will become storage for Christmas decorations and wrapping paper and Mom's winter sweaters. Boxes that are intended for the garage will more readily find a home on my shelves. It will always be *referred* to as my room, but shortly it will no longer be my room.

Warm and secure under my blanket this morning, the fear of leaving strangely began to smother the fear of not leaving. As desperately as I wanted to run from the small-town ways of this city, it hurt to leave behind my little family. Only two seemingly simple good-byes stood in the way of my leaving this morning, but I couldn't seem to move. I knew when my feet hit the ground I had to run and not look back. Move quickly, I figured. That's what years of taking off Band-Aids have taught me about avoiding pain.

My first good-bye after crawling out of bed was delivered into darkness through the crack in my brother's open door. The light that spilled onto his face woke him up.

"I'm leaving now; I just wanted to say good-bye," I said.

He lifted his groggy head and said, "Take care."

My brother is someone who doesn't ever talk and has virtually nothing in common with me. Todd has two words in his vocabulary: *Huh?* and *Idunno*, and one discernible emotion that he uses: *indifference*. So that simple offering of "Take care," coming from an otherwise emotionless individual, struck harder than a summer's worth of electrical storms. "Take care" almost brought me to my knees. I had never before considered whether I had been the best brother and father I could to him, but I think the "Take care" answered it for me. It was his gesture of appreciation for my dressing up as Santa every year at Christmas, letting him pin me when we wrestled on the lawn, and holding his bike seat for weeks after the training wheels had come off. I stumbled into the laundry room, trying to suppress my emotions. I didn't want Mom to interpret the tears as apprehension, or worse, that maybe I wasn't man enough to handle it. Propped up between the Sears washer and dryer, I made a strange and sobering discovery: I have never done a load of my own laundry. That will have to change.

Finally, the only thing that stood between me and saying good-bye to Mom was the screen door, a door I had gone in and out of a thousand different times for a thousand different reasons, but never had one caused me to stop and question my reason. I remember one childhood winter, in a haste to get outside and throw snowballs at passing cars or girls, my head ended up through the glass storm door, which put my mother in haste for the hospital and the doctor in haste for stitches. That accident proved to be one of my first memories of pain, the second being the day I tested my homemade parachute. There was a slight problem with the release mechanism in my Scooby-Doo backpack, and back then, ten feet was a long way to drop.

Our dog, Chancy, who we've had for four years, ran into the living room and received one last pat. As I rose to my feet, I realized the next trip through the door would bring with it much deeper pain than a two-inch laceration or a fall from the roof could ever inflict, pain that will now be served to me by life, not childhood; pain that can't be mended with a simple stitch or a motherly kiss.

Through the haze of the screen door and the rain that had begun to fall, I could see that Mom was organizing the trunk of my car, which I had spent four hours organizing the night before. Something like that would normally have enraged me, but I knew the busywork kept her mind off the fact that in a matter of minutes she'd be losing her firstborn child to the world.

The rain was soaking her, but she didn't seem to notice. With each box she shifted, my throat grew tighter and my heart sunk deeper. I could taste the hurt creeping up the back of my tongue like the contents of a septic tank bubbling its way to the surface. I wanted to give up. The want for "more" was suddenly gone. The only "want" left in me was to sit at the kitchen table with my family and have breakfast. Odd, when one considers the fact we had rarely, if ever, had breakfast as a family before.

Damn her, I thought. Why doesn't she realize I'm afraid? Why is she *re*packing and not *un*packing? I'm not taking another step.

And yet she continued.

I had no desire to step through the door. The pain was too great. But the man of the house in me knew the pain in her was far greater, and that it was my responsibility to take the initiative. As soon as my hand touched the handle, I would run for the car and avoid all eye contact, which I tried to do, but she stopped me with a question: "Anything else for the trunk?"

I couldn't answer. I couldn't even look at her. She gave me twenty-three years of her life and I was leaving her without a nod.

She continued, "Well, I think I have everything packed in there as good as I can. If I find anything else, we can always send it. Chancy and I get uptown a couple times a day. Of course Chance doesn't like the rain, so on those days we usually only make one trip, but he's got a vet appointment next Tuesday so I hope for his sake it doesn't rain."

There was no more room for my throat to strain. The more she kept telling me things I already knew, the harder it was to keep from bursting.

"Your gas tank is full so you shouldn't have to stop until Jamestown. And when you do, make sure they check the oil; that's their job. Which reminds me, someday I have to get your brother out here to change the oil in my car, I don't think it's been changed since June when we all went to the ..."

And with that she was done. I was done. There was no more energy left in either of us to continue the battle. We held each other tight. For the first time in years she had nothing to say. Our whimpering was the only thing audible.

Finally, she petted the back of my hair and said, "I'm going to miss you, son. I love you."

I couldn't imagine letting go, getting in my car, driving away, and leaving her to her tears ... but I did.

I remember looking in the rearview mirror and seeing Mom standing in the middle of the road, waving. Soaked. And as I turned the corner at the far end of the block, I saw her still waving.

Those are the thoughts and images that haunt me now as I sit in my car outside of Larson's Supermarket, perched on the border of my future.

I press the accelerator and pull away from the curb. I take a final look back in the mirror at the last evidence of civilization before hitting the highway and notice the town is beginning to bubble, and lives appear to be continuing without me. Funny, I had always assumed I was the reason the town existed, and I had hoped that the day I left, it would go dark and eventually be strangled by weeds to its final breath.

There is a sign at the end of the block that reads, "You are now leaving Fargo." A guy has to wonder if that's really necessary when the road ahead is surrounded by five hundred acres of wheat. As I drive past the sign, I can't help but think of Mom back home and wonder what she's doing. Is she still in the street waving? Part of me hopes she is—a wave that will sustain a connection between us forever. The chances are she's distracting herself with busywork: puttering around the kitchen, cleaning out the fridge, pouring a nearly empty bottle of salad dressing into another—"marrying them," she calls it—and oftentimes the dressings are two completely different flavors.

Perhaps she's baking Todd some brownies in an attempt to hold on tight to her remaining son. She has nothing to worry about with Todd, however; he's not going anywhere. He's a midwesterner through and through. He'll be married with three kids, have a secure job, and buy a house in the neighborhood before my car reaches the Rocky Mountains.

Maybe Mom is once again looking for a list she's lost—actually they're pieces of paper with only one item; she loses track of them before they technically become lists. The queasy pit of my stomach makes me think that whatever it is she's doing, she's probably dying inside as well. Leaving home is something a son shouldn't have to do to a mother. We should be able to simply awaken one day to find ourselves already gone, in a home of our own, with a warm breakfast on the table and a fresh coat of eggshell white, interior latex on the walls.

Something percolated in me this morning, a deep-seated realization about this town and the people in it that was revealed to me only after a trip down Sheyenne Street. It had never matched the lives and lifestyles that I saw on television, which was my only evidence of life outside of Fargo. It was as if I'd learned how to live by watching TV, and the people I was surrounded by every day were doing it wrong. But in twelve short blocks, things have shifted. Recollection upon recollections of characters and events that previously had felt like barbed protrusions digging into my life are now reverberating in my head, creating a comforting, compassionate chord.

These people weren't holding me back from dreaming; in fact, signs of encouragement were all around me. Melvin, the nebbish mechanic, wanted to embody Neil Diamond and accomplished it. *Do the best you can.* An elderly couple strove through the adversities of a childless marriage to find themselves developing, nurturing, and loving an entire town of kids who frequented their little ice-cream shop. *If you can't do what you love, find another way.* Is there any greater triumph than the son of a Lutheran minister surgically becoming a woman? *Do what you have to do, no matter what people think.*

I didn't see how important all these people and their endeavors were at the time, or what they represented. To me they were simply freaks or simpletons. The miles' and miles' worth of farmers tilling the land that was passed down through generations are all important. Helen, who taught my parents, and all the teachers over the years who have valued their jobs and taught me from a place of *caring*, are important. I realize now that these people are a part of me; they're behind my eyes, they're in my skin, and they're in my nails, my hair, and my heart. Being unable to embrace them would mean being unable to embrace myself. Good or bad, I would not be who I am today without them.

And tomorrow? I don't know what will be tomorrow. If I'm lucky, the work ethic and values of the people who make up the foundation of this town have permeated my being and will serve me in my adventures.

For now, a left on Main Street will take me out of town, and I-94 will take me out of the state. There is nothing but blue skies ahead, and I will revel in it. I will revel in the memories and the people. I will revel in the joy of Fargo.

APPENDIX
Recipes

Rhubarb bars (crisp)
2 cups oatmeal
2 cups brown sugar
2 cups flour
1 cup butter (melted)
Mix together
Add half contents to bottom of 9x13 pan. Pat down firmly to create a base.
Add 8 cups raw rhubarb (cubed)
1½ cups sugar cover
Add other half of crust mixture, creating a top layer
Add crushed walnuts to top
Bake 30 minutes at 350 degrees
Enjoy with whipped cream or ice cream!

Potato chip casserole
1 8-ounce package of egg noodles
Boil and drain
1 12-ounce can of corn beef
¼ pound of Velveeta cheese
1 can cream of chicken soup
1 cup milk (or more if needed)

½ cup chopped onion
Salt and pepper
Add contents to 9 × 13 pan, breaking up corn beef
Bake 45 minutes at 350 degrees, covered with foil
Add a layer of crushed potato chips on top and bake another 15 minutes, uncovered
Let cool
Enjoy!

Tater Tots Casserole
1 pound ground hamburger
3 cups diced celery
1 cup diced onion
1 can cream of mushroom soup
1 can cream of chicken soup
Brown hamburger in pan; drain grease
Put into 9 × 13 inch glass pan; mix well
Place bag of frozen Tater Tots on top
Bake 1 to 1½ hours at 350 degrees
Let cool
Enjoy!

Chex Mix
3 cups Corn Chex
3 cups Rice Chex
3 cups Wheat Chex
1 cup mixed nuts
1 cup pretzels (break into bite size)
1 cup bagel chips (break into bite size)
Put contents into large roaster pan and mix well
In separate pan melt:
6 tablespoons butter
2 tablespoons Worcestershire sauce
1½ teaspoons seasoning salt
¾ teaspoon garlic powder
½ teaspoon onion powder

Bake for 1 hour at 250 degrees
Stir every 15 minutes

Sour Cream Raisin Pie
1 cup raisins in some water, boil slowly until soft
Drain, add 1 cup sour cream
1 cup brown sugar
4 tablespoons flour
Dash of salt
Cook in pan on stove until thick
Beat 2 egg yolks and add to mixture
Heat till boiling; remove from stove
Add 1 teaspoon vanilla
Pour contents into pie crust
Bake 45–60 minutes at 350 degrees
Remove pie to cool and prepare meringue
¼ tablespoon salt
½ tablespoon vanilla
3 egg whites
6 tablespoons sugar
Add salt and vanilla to egg whites and beat until stiff foam
Add 1 tablespoon of sugar at a time while continually beating
Continue beating until mixture forms moist peaks
Spread over pie and bake at 350 degrees 12–15 minutes or until golden brown
Let cool
Enjoy!